Now What, Grad?

Other Books by Chris Palmer

Shooting in the Wild: An Insider's Account of Making Movies in the Animal Kingdom (Sierra Club Books, 2010)

Confessions of a Wildlife Filmmaker: The Challenges of Staying Honest in an Industry Where Ratings Are King (Bluefield Publishing, 2015)

~

All proceeds from the sale of this book will go to fund scholarships for students in the American University School of Communication who have overcome, or are overcoming, challenges and adversity in their lives, such as poverty, marginalization, racism, or personal tragedy.

Now What, Grad?

Your Path to Success After College

Chris Palmer

ROWMAN & LITTLEFIELD
Lanham • Boulder • New York • London

Published by Rowman & Littlefield
A wholly owned subsidiary of The Rowman & Littlefield Publishing Group, Inc.
4501 Forbes Boulevard, Suite 200, Lanham, Maryland 20706
www.rowman.com

Unit A, Whitacre Mews, 26-34 Stannary Street, London SE11 4AB

British Library Cataloguing in Publication Information Available

Library of Congress Cataloging-in-Publication Data is available on file.

ISBN 978-1-4758-2365-3 (hardcover)
ISBN 978-1-4758-2366-0 (paperback)
ISBN 978-1-4758-2367-7 (electronic)

∞™ The paper used in this publication meets the minimum requirements of
American National Standard for Information Sciences—Permanence of Paper
for Printed Library Materials, ANSI/NISO Z39.48-1992.

Printed in the United States of America

Dedicated to my wife, Gail

Contents

~

Preface

The greatest danger for most of us is not that our aim is too high and we miss it, but it is too low, and we reach it.

—Michelangelo

As the student came into my office, I immediately could see that something was wrong. She was pale, and her shoulders sagged. "Are you okay?" I asked.

"Not really," she said. "I'm graduating in two months and don't have a job. I've been looking everywhere and networking like crazy, but nothing is panning out for me. I can't find a job!"

One of my top students, Paige Jones was editor in chief of American University's newspaper, *The Eagle*, and a double major in journalism and international relations. She was a hard-working, accomplished student, but she was plagued by her biggest fear about the future: that she wouldn't be able to start a career when she graduated, that she would have failed. Overwhelmed by the difficulties facing her, she was exhausted after trying to navigate today's workplace. "It's scary to think I might graduate without a job despite all the hard work I put into my classes, my work, and *The Eagle*," she told me. Sadly, this student is not alone in feeling somewhat despondent as graduation from college approaches.

Another of my excellent students, Kevin Borow, a graduating senior who had double majored in film and business administration, told me that failing was also his greatest concern: "I fear being unable to find where I belong in this world and ending up in a position that isn't fulfilling."

Similarly, Jacob Motz, who double majored in film and political science and was yet another of my outstanding students, said that his fiercest anxieties focused on two possibilities—that he would not find work after graduation, or that he would, but his first job would fail to meet his ambitions. Jacob said, "One of the most significant things I've learned at AU is the importance of community. Each school, each fraternity, each club, each group of friends offers a safety net for life's disappointments and a platform to celebrate life's joys. You need a community to support you, to motivate you, and to love you in the good times and the bad." He worried that he wouldn't find that kind of community outside of college.

Berna Elibuyuk, another of my top graduate students, told me that soon after graduating, she began sending her résumé to all of the internship and part-time positions she could find that related to her major. She assumed she would be able at least to find a good internship position at a graphics company. Instead, she received e-mails and phone calls saying she was "potential" employee material but then lost out at the very end every time. "The roads to success were all paved before me, but as soon as I walked down one, I would end up right back where I started," she told me.

The constant job searches drained her mental and physical energy. Not only did she tire from filling out long applications and answering broad and lengthy job questions, but her emotional state flipped inside out. "I was in turmoil," she said. "I kept asking myself, 'Am I not good enough?' I was a grade-A student who produced quality work, so why wasn't I getting job offers? I felt stuck, with no ideas about what to do next."

Other students have told me:

- "I am deeply afraid that all of the effort, time, and investment my family has so generously placed in me will be wasted, and I will not achieve anything significant."
- "My biggest fear about the future is not being successful and failing to make it in the real world."
- "I'm afraid that the film industry won't understand who I am as a filmmaker."
- "My biggest worry is not ever finding out how I will impact the world and not doing anything worthy of me."
- "I'm terrified of graduating from college as a humanities major. I have no idea where I am going to be this time next year."

At a recent graduation ceremony, I asked the assembled students to put up their hands if they felt apprehensive about the future and worried that it may prove difficult and challenging. Virtually all raised their hands.

Far too many students and recent graduates like Paige, Kevin, Jacob, and Berna—and perhaps like you—are deeply worried about the future.

Those of us who teach can do a lot to help our students allay these fears by guiding them toward valuable technical skills. For example, in my field I can teach animation, cinematography, editing, interactive media, trans-media, participatory media, and immersive media. I can help build student competence on digital devices, social media, mobile apps, and augmented reality. I can work with maturing communications experts to create meaningful and purposeful media through visual and aural storytelling. Other fields offer their own unique sets of skills, techniques, and knowledge that professors can teach.

But in the real world, technical know-how alone does not ensure a successful career, not least because whatever technical skills a student possesses at graduation will soon be outdated. Young people need to learn how to succeed. They must sharpen their "soft" skills: how to collaborate; how to take initiative and be lifelong learners; how to be adaptable, resilient, and resourceful; how to be ambitious, confident, and assertive; and how to live with honor and integrity.

They must learn how to be professionals. Professionalism involves civility, courtesy, a solid work ethic, balance, networking, and strong communication skills. Professionals acknowledge and learn from mistakes, act as team players, consistently give their best effort, always treat others with respect, and keep their promises.

Our students must learn to be leaders. Leadership requires entrepreneurial and critical-thinking skills as well as discipline, focus, and competence in time management. A leader must be a skilled, persuasive communicator, ready to think big and boldly but also be ready to listen. Team-building skills, mentoring, and coaching also are vital.

Perhaps the most important characteristics of a leader are the ability to take initiative and to follow a moral compass. Students must seize opportunities and make things happen. They must be willing to work hard. They must learn how to serve as exceptional employees and how to run businesses wisely. They need to know how to persevere and stay focused despite setbacks and rejections. They should network relentlessly and effectively, so that they can find new opportunities and tap into the best financial resources.

Most importantly, students must know how to build and maintain long-term, happy, healthy, fulfilling relationships with other people based on mutual respect. They need to mold themselves into human beings with great integrity, trustworthiness, reliability, decency, ability, and a great work ethic, so that people want to work with them.

In journalist Paul Tough's best-selling book, *How Children Succeed*, he argues that simply teaching cognitive skills such as math and reading to young children isn't nearly enough. He contends that the most important things to develop in children are noncognitive skills, that is, character traits such as integrity, self-control, self-discipline, focus, resilience, efficiency, ambition, perseverance, and resourcefulness. What is true for children is also true for college students.

The failure of advanced education to teach students, especially graduating college seniors, the fundamentals of building a successful career marks a great shortcoming. Professors give students job skills but generally neglect to give them job-getting skills. I wrote this book to help young people like you develop the aptitude and proficiency necessary for success in the work world. In this text, I share the experiences of students and recent graduates while offering advice and practical tips for succeeding in the workforce and in life.

As for Paige, Kevin, Jacob, and Berna, before the end of the book I'll tell you how they are doing.

Acknowledgments

I am grateful to the many students and former students who have shared with me their fears, questions, and successes. Their stories in this book show that today's job market can pose a difficult challenge to new college graduates looking for work. But these stories also illustrate the resilience and resourcefulness that students practice in tackling these challenges head-on. I have been struck by the wisdom in their reflections on what they've learned and achieved.

I want to thank the many writers, thinkers, and leaders who have shaped my life, including Stephen Covey, Tony Robbins, Ben Franklin, Warren Bennis, Carl Sagan, Steve Allen, Victor Frankl, Isaac Asimov, Ambrose Bierce, Ira Byock, Mardy Grothe, Oscar Wilde, Brian Tracy, Atul Gawande, Nick Morgan, and many others. They have helped to inspire this book.

The specific impetus for this book came from the regular bimonthly essays, "Best Practices," that I write for *Realscreen* magazine. I'm grateful to the editor Barry Walsh for giving me the opportunity over the past six years to contribute on a regular basis to his excellent publication. I often sought the help of my American University teaching assistants in researching and drafting those essays, so I owe great thanks to Shannon Lawrence, Jazmin Garcia, Peter Kimball, Matt Lucas, Angeli Gabriel, and Scott Bastedo.

The idea for this book came from leading communications expert Diane MacEachern. Editor Megan Scribner played a big role in helping me think through how to organize the book. My youngest daughter, Jenny, gave me pivotal assistance in helping me present the contents in a logical way. Roger DiSilvestro did a superb job editing the text, and Sue Gordon from American University Career Center read the whole manuscript and gave me helpful comments. I thank Diane, Megan, Jenny, Roger, and Sue profusely for their help and guidance.

I'm also very grateful to Tom Koerner and his team at Rowman & Littlefield for believing in the book and publishing it.

Finally, let me thank the various students who generously contributed their stories to this book. You'll see their names scattered throughout the text, but let me list them here to express my gratitude: Susan Billings, Kevin Borow, Janetta Depeppa, Berna Elibuyuk, Erin Finicane, Alexander Gillies, Vanina Harel, Paige Jones, Shannon Lawrence, Jacob Motz, Will Reid, Sam Sheline, Urjita Sudula, Susie Vulpas, and Nick Zachar.

My family is a continual source of joy and inspiration. I'm deeply grateful to my wonderful wife, Gail, my three amazing daughters (Kimberly, Christina, and Jenny), my two outstanding sons-in-law (Sujay and CJ), and my three adorable grandchildren (Kareena, Neal, and Jackson).

~

Introduction

> [W]e don't educate our children at school; we stultify them and then send them out into the world half baked. And why? Because we keep them utterly ignorant of real life. The common experience is something they never see or hear.
>
> —Suetonius

The failure of schools to teach students about the challenges they will face upon graduation is an age-old problem—the quote above is from one of the world's earliest novels, *The Satyricon*, written nearly two thousand years ago.

I won't pretend that my slim volume, *Now What, Grad?*, will correct a problem that has plagued the world for millennia, but if you are a recent grad, or are about to be a grad, or are engaged in any way, shape, or form in entering the world of careers and professions, this book may solve some important problems for you.

Although the chapters build on one another and are arranged in a sequence designed to give a certain order to how you prepare for and approach your opening assault on the job market, you can jump into the book at any point and find that the chapters stand largely alone, offering advice on critical aspects of your evolving role as a professional.

Part I: Reflect on Your Life opens with the big questions—what do you want from life and how do you correlate your actions with your goals and values to start on the way to the career you want.

Part II: Land a Job delves into the practical aspects of seeking work. It will help you to chart a course across the hazards and challenges of a job search, focus on the skills you possess, and guide you toward being a highly desirable employee. You will find practical advice on how to engage in interviews that will highlight your strengths, how to avoid the worst mistakes in job searches, and how to heighten your originality and appeal in seeking and finding a job.

Part III: Maximize Your Productivity focuses on making you into a career champion. You'll read about one of the key elements of a successful career—time management—which translates into efficiency. You will learn to control e-mail, one of the great time sinks, rather than let it control you. You will even find directions for making yourself a more vital and fit individual, energized to meet the challenges you are going to face.

Part IV: Communicate Effectively deals with interpersonal skills, a central part of professional success. Communication skills are critical to leadership and networking as well as a means, through public speaking, to build your credentials. In this section you will learn how to speak effectively and to tell stories that hold an audience or an individual's attention. It shows you how to lead panel discussions, run productive meetings, and create a courteous and sincere work environment.

Part V: Make Meaningful Connections examines networking. No one is an island—as you may have heard—which makes building professional relationships vitally important to your success. After you read this section, you will have the basics for describing your professional skills, goals, and purposes in a few brief sentences. You will be equipped to master the craft of networking, which can yield lifelong relationships of mutual respect and assistance. And you'll learn the fundamentals of fund-raising, a skill so important that those who have it are better positioned than those who don't for success in any career. Money, some say, makes the world go round; being able to raise money for your activities or for the organization for which you work makes a career take off like a rocket.

Now What, Grad? offers two appendixes that should prove useful to you and that shouldn't be ignored. In the early pages of the book, you will learn about the importance of writing a personal mission statement that will serve as your life map. Appendix A offers excerpts from the mission statements of several of my students as well as my own mission statement, which I have polished and honed across several decades. Appendix B is the text of a handout for a workshop I give that outlines fifty ways to be a stronger person and a more dynamic professional. It recaps many of the points made in the various chapters, making it a one-stop resource to help you create shortcuts to a rewarding career.

I hope you'll find *Now What, Grad?* a useful companion and guide as you chart your progress through the various stages of work and life. As I mentioned earlier, you can read it all the way through or pick it up as needed—whatever works best for you. Thank you for letting me join you as you begin the often turbulent journey into the professional world.

~

PART I

REFLECT ON YOUR LIFE

The best use of life is to spend it for something that outlasts life.

—William James

I'm at a loss for what to do after college. I don't know what I want to be when I "grow up"—much less what I want or should do right after graduation! What do I want to do? Who do I want to be? What is my life about? What is my purpose? How do I want to be remembered? What's my next step? Job or graduate school or travel? Where do I want to live? How do I begin to figure it out?

1

CHAPTER ONE

~

Life after College,
a Time of Transition

The tragedy of life doesn't lie in not reaching your goal. The tragedy lies in having no goal to reach.

—Benjamin Mays

Leaving college and stepping out on your own can lead to seemingly over-whelming challenges. Suddenly the rules, assignments, and deadlines you once resented and struggled against are gone. But so is the structure that gave order and shape to your activities, goals, and life.

Now you may seem to face too many choices, too many options. You may be longing for someone to tell you what to do, to set you on the right path and give you a push! No one can do that for you, but it is a challenge that you can meet successfully if you practice a few essential skills that are easily taught and almost as easily mastered. These skills can make the challenge more exciting and exhilarating and less scary. Think of it this way: the world is in front of you, and this is your chance to step out boldly and embrace your future.

Erin Finicane, a recent graduate from American University, explains three major, challenging transitions she and her friends experienced after leaving college:

Social-Life Transition

In college, you are constantly surrounded by people your age. You have a built-in network of friends and people who can stimulate you intellectually and socially. Leaving college and being very suddenly thrown into the real world where you have to build a new network of friends and colleagues from scratch is overwhelming and often a slow process. Many of my friends have had issues with depression that come from a feeling of social isolation and loneliness. That in turn impacts their productivity, motivation, and self-confidence.

Life-Structure Transition

Similar to confronting the social-life transition, students graduating from college go from having their entire lives scheduled and structured (whether by their parents or by school) to suddenly having little or no structure and having to figure it all out on their own.

In school, students have short- and long-term work goals based on the deadlines and requirements of their classes or degrees. Clubs and student organizations offer them a built-in channel for pursuing what they are passionate about. They have extracurricular activities readily available to them. Upon graduating and losing that built-in infrastructure, students realize just how much they take for granted and how much of their lives have been scheduled for them.

Intellectual Freedom

One of the other things I've personally experienced, and have talked about at length with friends who have gone through it, is the transition in intellectual stimulation and creative freedom. Throughout our student careers, we've been encouraged to stretch our minds, be creative, and explore what we find intellectually stimulating.

When we leave college and enter the workforce, there seems to be no space for these practices, at least not in the initial entry-level jobs we find ourselves occupying. Many friends find themselves just pushing numbers, doing PowerPoint, running in and out of meetings, and generally getting caught in a routine that isn't particularly stimulating. And for some, despite working their way up, it doesn't seem that their work will ever get all that stimulating—instead, their baseline for what they consider satisfactory just gets lower.

> When I was graduated from college, I was hit with a feeling of what I can describe only as terror. I stood on a precipice in my life, not knowing what the next steps would or should be. — Urjita Sudula, recent grad student

While navigating these drastic social, structural, and intellectual transitions, recent college graduates such as Erin also are trying to find and keep jobs. The economy has changed a great deal in the past few years, but for anyone new to the career world, today indeed marks a challenging time.

My goal was to get a summer internship. I applied for one at a television production company that I admired, contacting them through their website. I didn't hear anything back for months. They did not list a contact number or any way to follow up on the application. I was getting frustrated as I couldn't really make other plans until I heard back from them. I started talking to my professors about it, and one of them introduced me by e-mail to a woman at the company. She suggested I come to a networking event.

By the time I found my contact and her supervisor at the event, they were surrounded by a crowd of students, making it hard to speak with them individually. However, at the end of the event I was able to speak with both when no one else was around. I was very honest about what I was looking for and interested in.

I followed up with e-mails to both of them, thanking them for their time and asking them to let me know if they had any opportunities for the summer. A couple of weeks later, they e-mailed me about two temporary positions. Neither assignment was appealing to me, but I was excited to have an opportunity and went in for an interview. From what I gathered, they just wanted to get to know me and to introduce me to their team. I left without knowing what to think.

Two weeks later, I received an e-mail asking me if I was still interested in a summer internship. I responded warmly and positively. About an hour later, an e-mail from the human-resources department told me the internship was mine.

I could not believe it. I was lucky to have been there at a time when the position opened up and to have had a good recommendation from one of my professors. My future colleagues seemed to have liked me as a person, even though I did not have the technical skills required for the opening.

Though I was interning in a department I knew was not for me, I managed to take full advantage of my time. I met the heads of every department and learned about the world of television production. I made great contacts and figured out which department would be more suitable for my interests and skills. It was an invaluable experience and showed me that persevering and taking the position that is offered, even if it doesn't seem like quite the right fit, can sometimes pay off. I also learned that although skills are important, employers also are looking for people who are professional and with whom they think they can work. Moreover, every applicant comes with a great degree and work experience, so a good reference from close contacts can make the deal. —Vanina Harel, grad student

Don't despair. Lessons are here to be learned, experiences to be gained. What you learn now—through all the challenges of your budding career—will be the most important building blocks to the life and profession that await you. Take time now to reflect on who you are and what you want to do. You've taken a great first step in reading this book.

As you work on your career, please remember to take care of the other important aspects of your life. Keep doing the activities that make you happy and keep you healthy and balanced. Be sure to make time for exercise and connecting with friends (the subject of upcoming chapters). Be very intentional about building friendships, and don't treat them like an afterthought. Be patient with yourself, and remember joy can be found in all stages of life—including the most challenging ones.

CHAPTER TWO

~

Align Your Actions with Your Values

Whatever you can do, or dream you can do, begin it. Boldness has genius, power, and magic in it.

—Goethe

The key to having a happy and successful life is finding out who you want to be and what you want to do—the big picture of your life—and then discovering the small details and steps that will lead you to your goals. This approach will keep you from feeling overwhelmed by the endless task of building a career and a profession. Breaking the immense challenge before you into measurable and manageable steps allows you to focus on the process and make consistent progress toward your goals without being paralyzed by the magnitude of the overall operation.

Many people never identify what they are passionate about. Fortunately, you can be different. Devote some thought to recognizing what aspects of career, friendship, family, politics, and other factors appeal to you most deeply. Take the feelings you discover within yourself and articulate them in words—what is the basis for your emotions and passions? What actions can you take that align with these intense feelings? Turning your feelings into a clearly stated understanding of them will give you a major piece of self-knowledge that many are missing and will help you to live a fulfilling life.

Make sure you care about something that is worth caring about. We all know people who care deeply about following certain reality shows on television. That doesn't mean that watching the programs and reading about the characters on gossip websites is a good use of time. Your thoughts, intellect, goals, values, and comprehension of yourself and of the people and activities around you can only match the quality of the knowledge and information you put into your brain. Set time aside for light entertainment, but do it consciously, so you will not compulsively and unknowingly become mired in hours and hours of wasted investment in activities that will not bolster and inform your understanding of the larger world.

Figuring out who you want to be and what you want to do can be hard to accomplish. Don't worry—you don't need to have the ultimate answers just yet. Since the distant time of earliest civilization, philosophers and leaders have struggled through the long process of knowing themselves. If done right, life is a long process of discovery—not just about people, places, and things, but about yourself. Just beginning to reflect on these questions will help you figure out your next steps and how they might fit into the larger picture of your life.

> After graduation, I secured an internship at a marketing firm that offered a wonderful opportunity to gain invaluable experience. I was learning so much. However, I was never excited to go to work. In fact, I dreaded it! At first I didn't understand my reaction. I had a job working with great people in a field that I enjoyed studying during college. So why didn't I love going to work every day?
>
> Through lots of self-reflective journaling, I learned what I was missing. As part of my job, I spent forty-plus hours building schedules and tracking budgets, but I wasn't creating anything of value or helping anyone in the world. In addition, I felt no passion about the work I was doing.
>
> During college, I enjoyed studying marketing and just assumed that I would enjoy a career in that field. However, I soon realized that I needed more than just a marketing job to feel fulfilled. I needed to be doing meaningful work for which I felt a passion. I wanted to be able to go home after a day at work and know that I had made a difference. I wish that I had reflected more on my values and what is important to me before I began my job search. If I had, I might have come to this realization sooner and altered my job search to find work in an area that I am passionate about. —Recent grad student

An important tool for making sense of all that you face now, that you will face in the future, and that you want to achieve in your career is your *personal mission statement*. Developing a personal mission statement will help give your life focus and help you decide at critical moments what to do with your time and energy. With this focus, you will be able to devote your time to what is most important to you and be on your way to a happy, fulfilling life.

Your personal mission statement is a chance to set goals for a lifetime. With any journey, having a roadmap to your destination is key to arriving where you want to go. Think of your mission statement as that roadmap. What do you want to achieve? How do you want to be remembered? For instance, you might write (as I did in my own personal mission statement), "I want to be remembered by my family, friends, and colleagues as a person grounded in decency, simple goodness, and inspiring enthusiasm. Someone with a lasting and wonderful marriage, a great sense of humor, and a strong work ethic."

The following chapter, based on Stephen R. Covey's excellent book, *The Seven Habits of Highly Effective People*, will help you begin to develop your own personal mission statement. You will want to hone it over the years and update it regularly. As life changes you, and you change life, your personal mission statement will become a living document that adapts with you to the pleasures and the plights that life puts in your path.

I often tell people that I learned more in the few years after college than during the four years I spent in college. After graduation, I was confident that I was going to find a job in the art world that connected with my passion for social, economic, and environmental justice. But then the economy crashed, I struggled to find work that left me satisfied, and I was forced to reconsider my goals when the work I had dreamed of just wasn't available.

Although there were a number of fields in which I could see myself working, there wasn't one, single path I could follow to reach them. This realization was horrifying and stressful. I applied for jobs in a number of fields without having a sense whether they would lead to the "right" path for me. I tried to imagine myself working in these fields and took on volunteer projects to try things out and to gain experience. I was engaged in real-world trial and error—a slow process that revealed what I was capable of, what I was drawn to, and what was possible.

Looking back, I don't think that writing a single mission statement would have eliminated the importance of this process for me, but a mission statement might have helped me with the process. As I learned from my experiences, I would have changed the portion of the statement that focused on the core personal values underlying all my choices and experiences. The expectations that students have in college do not always match the interests of the real world. Any tool, such as a personal mission statement, that can aid graduates in understanding what they want out of life is valuable in bridging that gap. —Will Reid, grad student

CHAPTER THREE

~

Develop Your Personal
Mission Statement

The best opportunities in life are the ones we create. Goal setting provides for you the opportunity to create an extraordinary life.

—Gary Ryan Blair

This chapter will help you develop your personal mission statement. Take time to think carefully about the questions here. Write down your answers in a journal or another place where you will be able to keep what you've written.

Be expansive and imaginative. Don't be overly modest, and don't let fears or anxieties keep you from setting your sights high or from pursuing what you are truly passionate about. Your statement will be a unique, detailed list of your most-valued principles, roles, relationships, and goals. It is the story of your interests and objectives and a forecast of the life you want to lead.

The first step in writing a mission statement is deciding what matters most to you. Think in both the short and long term. Be as specific as you can. Possibilities include finding a job that is meaningful and satisfying, finding a partner, balancing your work and personal life, earning enough money to support yourself, earning enough money to support a family, developing your sense of humor, being helpful, being kind, being happy, giving yourself to others, volunteering, saving the environment for future generations, being involved in a social-justice cause, and so forth.

Now think about the principles and values that are most important to you. What do you imagine is key to living a good life? Do you want to be remembered as an honest person? A kind person? A passionate person?

The next step is to identify your most important roles—your fundamental relationships and your responsibilities within those relationships. For example, your role as a mother, father, friend, son, daughter, sister, or brother, as an artist, entrepreneur, filmmaker, or activist, as a soccer coach or team member. Pick no more than seven roles so you can focus on those most crucial to you.

Now identify the people who are most important to you in regard to each of the roles you've named. What kind of relationship do you want with those people? What are the assessments you would like them to make about you at the end of your life? What actions do you need to take to build and sustain this kind of relationship?

Make sure that one of the roles in your life involves embracing self-development and renewal. You have to take care of yourself before you can take care of anybody or anything else. Self-renewal has four dimensions:

1. *Physical*, including fitness, exercise, strength, flexibility, endurance, eating healthily, getting enough sleep, and deep relaxation;
2. *Social/emotional*, including love, friendship, connecting with others, volunteering, helping people, and developing a sense of belonging;
3. *Mental*, including study, learning, reading, visiting museums and science centers, solving puzzles, writing, and evolving intellectually; and
4. *Spiritual*, including art, contemplation, poetry, finding a purpose and meaning in your life through service to others, going on a personal retreat to reflect on your life, being at one with nature, identifying long-range goals, studying your family history, leaving a legacy, or doing whatever is necessary to create joy and passion for you personally.

By identifying your roles, you create a variety of perspectives from which to examine your life and ensure balance. It is easy for us to focus on work so intensely that we lose sight of why we wanted to become successful at work in the first place. Being aware of your roles outside of work keeps your life in balance. Having a happy home life, for example, should be among your highest goals. You need consciously to take care of your health, your significant other, your friends, and your family. Restorative rest, relaxation, and leisure are important. Even star athletes don't train all day every day.

Finally, articulate some long-range goals that will help you achieve the life that you have imagined for yourself. Make sure to think about goals in your professional life, in your personal life, and in the four self-development/renewal dimensions. If you are having a hard time thinking of specific goals, you may want to take some time to brainstorm any possible jobs, roles, and activities that come to mind as you think about your life.

Now that you have recorded your life goals, the people important to achieving them, the roles you play in your world, and the other items mentioned above, you have the beginnings of a personal mission statement. Remember, there is no single, "correct" way of writing a personal mission statement. Yours need not look like anyone else's. Your mission statement can be as short as one sentence, or it can number several pages. It often takes time to find the words that inspire and excite you, to excavate from the depths inside you the roles you play and want to play, the activities and purposes that truly excite you, the difference between what you want from yourself and what you think others expect from you.

At this point, you may not feel you have the full picture of who you want to be. That's fine. Your personal mission statement will evolve over time and through experience. In fact, you should revisit it at regular intervals—several times a year—to edit or add to it. Periodically reviewing and revising it will ensure that you are still on track and effectively using your time to become the person you want to be. The process itself is as important as the "finished" product.

You can find some examples of personal mission statements in appendix A. Read them and use them as guides when you create your own. But remember that they are only examples. Each person's statement will reflect his or her individual goals and life as well as personality, attitudes, and insights.

Once you have a working personal mission statement, use it. As discussed in the chapter on managing time effectively, break up your long-term goals into more manageable, shorter-range goals. Plan your weekly and daily tasks to accomplish these shorter-range goals, and you will be on your way to achieving the longer-term ones.

Sometimes writing a five-year plan or all-encompassing life statement can seem overwhelming. I try to break down my goals into shorter time periods to give me a sense of accomplishment and forward movement. My goals to learn about filmmaking include weekly and monthly goals to work with camera equipment and to try out different editing techniques. —Shannon Lawrence, grad student

Remember that each day is important and should not be wasted. Every day that passes means you have one day less to live. The secret of your life and your future lies hidden in your daily routine. Derive what you are committed to do on a daily basis from the commitments in your personal mission statement rather than from the torrential flood of e-mails, meetings, interrup-

When I was in college and right after I graduated, I said yes to any videography job I could find. Anytime friends had a play or wedding they wanted filmed, I'd do it. As a result, I ended up with a mountain of editing work. I couldn't meet deadlines, because I'd taken on so much work. My reliability as a videographer went downhill. After I learned to look realistically at my schedule and say, "I don't have time to do that," my work and my professional relationships improved. —Alexander Gillies, grad student

tions, and so on that tend to distract you from what matters most to you. In this way, you can live each day true to your values, goals, and passions. When your daily actions match your personal mission statement, you will have achieved an important level of personal integrity.

PART II

~

LAND A JOB

We act as though comfort and luxury were the chief requirements of life, when all that we need to make us really happy is something to be enthusiastic about.

—Charles Kingsley

How do I get organized to find a job? Where should I start? What skills do I have that could possibly interest an employer? I haven't had many job interviews and they make me so nervous—how can I do better in them? What if I'm totally stuck and I just don't know what to do with my life?

~

CHAPTER FOUR

Organize Your Job Search

The act of taking the first step is what separates the winners from the losers.

—Brian Tracy

Whether you are just starting out, looking for new opportunities, or practicing as a freelance professional, when it comes to finding a new job in the current market, it's easy to get frustrated, disillusioned, and just plain exhausted. Stay positive. You are not alone.

When I started looking for jobs after college, I was immediately overwhelmed. I was not quite sure what I was qualified to do, and I was not exactly sure what I wanted to do. I started to search large, online, job databases and soon got frustrated with not finding interesting prospects. I also felt increasingly that my skills were inadequate even to apply for most positions.

I soon received advice that I should apply to any job I was interested in, because the worst that could happen was "No." If I never took the risk to apply, I would never know what opportunities I may have missed. With this in mind, I began to apply to more positions and felt less discouraged about not receiving replies for every single application. I scored more interviews and, eventually, a job. —Shannon Lawrence, grad student

The following ideas will expand your search methods and help you land a job:

- *Get organized.* Using your personal mission statement and its associated long-term and short-term goals, write out your plan of attack for finding a job. Write down all the people you will contact, all the websites you will look at, and all the networking events you will attend. Make your goals specific. Write "apply for three jobs today" instead of "look for jobs today." For more on how to develop your short-term goals and tasks, see chapter 10 on managing your time effectively.
- *Track your progress.* When you take an action, such as contacting a particular person or applying for a certain job, keep a clear record of it. This practice of recording your efforts will hold you accountable to your goals and help you keep track of what you've done so you don't waste time repeating your efforts later on.
- *Get online, now!* Skip the mega-job-search engines that yield thousands of listings and no results. Look for websites that cater to your industry. Search for people who have the job you want, and find out what they did to get it. You can get the scoop on your dream job while polishing your networking skills.
- *Narrow your search.* "Any job will do" is not the right attitude to maintain while searching for your next career opportunity. Go back to your personal mission statement and look again at the questions you answered during the exercise in chapter 3: What field or career are you passionate about? What skills do you have? What's next on your learning curve? What activities would you like to undertake at your next position?
- *Network relentlessly.* Schmoozing. Chitchatting. Socializing. Whatever you want to call it, you need to network. Your area offers plenty of opportunities. Look into professional associations connected with your field of study. Ask your professors for advice about which organizations, networks, and associations to approach. Talk to the career-services office at your college about individuals and associations that might be helpful. Remember that alumni offices and associations are great networking resources. Find two or three associations or networks that fit you. Go to their websites, keep up with their local news and happenings, and try to attend their meetings and conferences. Attend a gathering with other industry professionals in your area. See chapter 24 for more tips on networking.

- *Research. Research. Research.* Find out everything you can about the company to which you are applying. Not only will this information help you to match your skills with their needs in your cover letter and résumé, but it also will tell you if the company is a good fit for you.
- *Read carefully.* Be certain to read job descriptions thoughtfully, comparing your skills and activities list with the job duties. For instance, beginning filmmakers may find they have multiple talents, from reading scripts to shooting B-roll. Identify your skills—considering the full range of your experience at school and in your work and personal life—and use those skills to your advantage.
- *Be fresh, innovative, and enthusiastic in your cover letter.* Someone with a dull cover letter has about as good a chance as someone without any skills or talent. You want to appear enthusiastic about your potential future job. Stay professional, but set yourself apart from other applicants.

What assets do you have that would benefit the company in ways they haven't even considered? Perhaps you have started a side business making furniture or have coached a softball team. Think of several ways your hobbies contribute to your job skills, especially those that demonstrate leadership. Review your skill list (see chapter 5) and identify all of those that apply to this situation. Think of how you might speak to these in a cover letter or interview. Keep the contents of the cover letter relevant to the employer and the position. Then:

- *Prepare rigorously for your interview.* Preparation is key for any job interview. Practice beforehand with a friend or significant other, making sure you are ready for anything. Be sure to read the chapter on how to ace job interviews.
- *Dress for success.* The old adage is still relevant, but don't think that means you need to wear an expensive suit to your interview. The environment should dictate what you wear. Wearing a suit to a punk-band audition can be just as imprudent as wearing jeans and a T-shirt to a law-clerk interview. Ask during your phone interview what style of attire is appropriate for the office and dress one step up. Appear serious but not pretentious.
- *Show your passion during the interview and stay positive.* Keep in mind the reasons you want to work for the company and state them with enthusiasm. You want to show that you have a passion for the company's work, not just a yearning for a paycheck. A well-placed line regarding the company's last major breakthrough shows you care without appear-

When I first graduated and began seeking work in the art world, I attended many art openings dressed for success in the classic sense. This was, in retrospect, a mistake. The art buyers who attended these gallery openings dressed nicely. But the other artists, the people who could help me find work, generally did not. Dressing in suits made me stand out—and not in a good way. Many artists were surprised to learn that I was a painter. This problem could be cleared up easily through conversation, but the initial impression I made presented an additional barrier for me to overcome. With time, I learned to attend these events dressing like myself—and the other artists. —Will Reid, grad student

ing desperate. On the same note, it is crucial not to denigrate previous employers. No one wants to hire a disloyal person. If you left your previous job under bad terms, try to put a positive spin on the situation.

- *Remember to follow up.* After your interview, send a note thanking the hiring manager. Keep it polite, but acknowledge that you want the job and highlight the reasons you would be a good fit. Think of it as an additional cover letter, the one landing you the job rather than the interview.

When you are fresh out of college, leaving behind an environment where you felt that your creativity would be recognized and that your innovative ideas would be well received, you find yourself suddenly in the real world, where you must compete with people whose training and education is much like yours but tempered with what may be years of experience. They have learned the practicalities of the workday world, its limitations and demands.

Don't feel discouraged if these practicalities feel tedious and if you feel that your skills are unrecognized. Nothing can magnify that discouragement and those feelings more than the process of job hunting, which can arguably serve as a metaphor for tedium. Filling out applications, going through interviews, feeling put on the spot are hurdles that all employed people have had to leap. You can do it too, and you will.

It is true that demonstrating passion is a wonderful way to find a job. I once landed a job by showing up at the business in a suit with a résumé in hand even though a job wasn't available at the time. As it turned out, someone quit a few months after I visited, and the manager remembered that I had come by—something he would later tell me had impressed him. —Will Reid, grad student

Review the advice in this chapter periodically, especially after an interview. Check to see how your experience matched the advice here, and examine honestly any areas in which you may have fallen short. Above all, hang in there, because once you land your first career job, you have overcome perhaps the most challenging obstacle in your professional path.

CHAPTER FIVE

~

Create Your Skill List

Use the talents you possess, for the woods would be a very silent place if no birds sang except the best.

—Henry van Dyke

When compiling a list of your skill sets, be creative! Think beyond the typical job description and your traditional jobs. Consider all your work, your volunteer efforts, even your collaborative experiences in the classroom. Consider the skills and qualities that you needed for each effort and how they might apply in the workforce generally. One colleague of mine, early in his career, put on his résumé his experience managing a family woodlot in the Adirondacks.

Create your skill list now—before your next job interview—so you have a wide range of skills and descriptive words that you can draw from for cover letters, résumés, or interviews. You may not mention all these skills in an interview or cover letter, but knowing that you have them will enable you to respond to questions with confidence.

Ask yourself questions in the following four areas:

1. *Leadership*: What leadership roles have you had? What did you learn from these experiences? What did the successes and failures teach you about yourself and your talents and skills? What are your leadership skills? For instance, are you well organized? Do you like being in charge, or are you

better at taking instructions and then running with them? All of these are valuable skills if seen and described in the right way.

2. *People skills*: Are you a good team player? Are you a people person, or do you like to work behind the scenes? Do you like to collaborate? What experience do you have from being part of an organization, a sports team, a theater troupe, a social group—or even a dorm—that illustrates your ability to work with people?

3. *Knowledge and expertise*: What jobs, volunteer efforts, and college assignments are relevant to the work or career you'd most like to have? What experiences are relevant to jobs you might apply for while waiting for the "perfect" job? List all the skills and knowledge you needed to get previous jobs and what you gained while doing them.

   Think about all the aspects of the work you did and how you responded to them. At what parts did you excel? What parts kept you up at night? As you look back, what do your responses tell you about yourself? What do they say about your talents, about what you're drawn to, about what tasks you'd rather not do? All these insights are helpful to you in searching for the right job and in positioning yourself as a good candidate for employment.

4. *Technical know-how*: What technical skills do you have? Create a personal list of all your skills, such as computer know-how, online dexterity, Web development and management, data entry, editing, writing, producing or editing videos, photography, and film. List them all, no matter how mundane they may seem. Some organizations do not have a high-tech component. For these organizations, your ability to create PowerPoints or Excel sheets could be very valuable.

Once you have thoroughly examined your skill set, practice describing each of your skills in three to five sentences, so that you will be prepared to discuss your talents quickly and concisely during an interview. If you do so, you will demonstrate both your technical abilities and your communications skills.

Be prepared to give specific examples of where and how you applied your skills, showing your practical knowledge and your ability to implement your proficiency at particular tasks and situations. You can facilitate this discussion by studying the needs of the company to which you are applying prior to an interview, as discussed previously. Familiarity with the company will allow you to highlight your skills in a way that appeals most to the interviewer.

CHAPTER SIX

~

Be Super-Employable

I am not a product of my circumstances. I am a product of my decisions.

—Stephen R. Covey

To survive in today's economy you must do everything in your power to make yourself *super*-employable. As earlier chapters have stressed, at a basic level employers want to hire people with academic credentials and work experiences that match the needs of the job. When you're first starting out, it can seem difficult to acquire the necessary skills, but you can develop these fundamentals in many ways throughout your life and through your schooling and jobs.

To be super-employable at this basic level, gain as much knowledge and experience as you can:

- Once you've compiled your list of skills as described in the previous chapter, build on that list. Identify weaknesses and gaps and fill them. Develop special skills that are valuable to employers: learn Chinese, computer programming, or film editing using the latest software.
- Pursue internships and entry-level positions to gain experience. Employers naturally prefer to hire candidates who already have relevant skills and knowledge of the industry. Many entry-level positions require experience—a sort of catch-22—making it difficult to find employment when starting out. Internships, including unpaid internships, are a great way to get your foot in the door.

For many students, unpaid internships are out of the question. They may lack parents who can fund them while they acquire experience in unpaid jobs. One recourse is to find, in addition to an internship, a second, paying "survival job," such as waiting tables in a restaurant, or serving as a barista at Starbucks.

Perhaps you can do as one aspiring young photographer did when he wanted to go to Europe for a year. He worked two jobs for at least a year, one as an assistant at a national conservation group and one as a sales clerk at a clothing store, until he had saved enough money to spend a year roughing it in Europe, where he found a job in construction for extra cash. Now, thirty years later, he is still in Europe, working as a videographer on international cruises for a German ship line. He's been around the world at least half a dozen times.

- Another way to gain experience is to get some freelancing gigs under your belt. Again, you might start out with unpaid projects or work for family and friends.
- Consider completing a master's degree in a field that you want to pursue as a career. A specialized degree will expand your skill set as well as demonstrate to employers that you are committed to the field. However, don't rush into this decision—graduate school costs a lot of money, and after graduation you might find yourself job hunting once again—but with more debt.

You may be thinking that at this point in your life and career, it is impossible to dramatically change your knowledge base and work experience.

When I graduated, I took a temporary position doing data entry (something boring that I had little interest in) for a science-focused conservation nonprofit (the exact industry I wanted a job in). After three months of working hard, being friendly, and generally doing a good job as a data-entry person, I was invited to work at the company's home office in an entirely different role. Although I still had to interview with my boss-to-be, it was only a formality. They recognized my skills and wanted me to work for them.

What led to this success? I believe it was because I had a diverse skill set: I was a biology major, which helped me relate to the science-intensive focus of the organization, but I also had film and electronic-media experience. They were looking for that mix of scientific understanding and film-production experience. This combination, along with doing a good job in an entry-level position, opened the door to doing exactly what I wanted—film production at a reputable environmental nonprofit. —Sam Sheline, grad student

You may not want to go back to school. In that case, focus on the areas over which you do have control. Here are three ways you can make this work for you:

1. *First, demonstrate your passion and drive to potential employers.* Passion can be shown through volunteering for relevant projects or completing your own projects, such as filming and editing your own movie. Employers want to see an entrepreneurial spirit that will continue to motivate you if they hire you. Having a genuine interest in a profession and the motivation to learn about it—despite the lack of pay—is something employers value and could make any applicant an attractive candidate for a paid position.

2. *Second, actively network.* As I'll say throughout this book (and especially in Chapter 24), networking is invaluable. Making new business friends can lead to fresh ideas, useful information, new partnerships, and, of course, new jobs. Networking will give you connections to potential employers and could provide references during the application process. Networking is about building relationships and trust. It is an essential skill for professionals who want to grow their careers. To network successfully, be authentic, unselfish, and honest. See the chapter on giving elevator speeches for more tips on networking.

3. *Finally, pay attention to the details to make sure you are always putting your best foot forward.* When you begin your job search, spruce up your online presence just as you would put on the proper clothing for an interview. If you're on Facebook and other social media sites, remove all photos that might be deemed unprofessional, such as you looking tipsy at a party and behaving inappropriately. All writings, blog posts, photos, and so forth by and about you should reflect the utmost professionalism.

Make sure your cover letter and résumé have absolutely no errors—even typos can be a deal breaker. Be aware that errors in letters occur most often in the addresses, titles, and names at the top of the first page. Ask someone you trust to review these documents for you. When you network and interview, have a strong handshake and smile genuinely: these small details can make a huge difference.

Keep in mind that job interviews are themselves a form of networking. One journalist who came to Washington, D.C., looking for a position with a conservation group knocked on the doors of the organizations for which he wanted to work, even though he was not aware of any job openings. After

I've found that confidence (or the appearance of it) goes a long way. Fake it until you make it—as the old adage goes—is an effective behavior. I don't mean to say that we should lie or be boastful. But I have certainly found that hiding my fears and insecurities has brought me more opportunities. Even when I am learning how to do something for the first time, I try to project a sense of confidence about my ability to figure it out and do a good job. I've found that more often than not, I can handle any task I'm given—at least well enough and without correction. Having this kind of confidence—or appearance of it—makes all the difference with coworkers and supervisors. Because I assume I can succeed, they do too. —Will Reid, grad student

three days of this activity, one editor with whom he interviewed referred him to another editor at another group, who told him to see a third editor who had an opening at yet another group—the one at which the neophyte journalist most wanted to work. He landed that job, and it was the start of a thirty-year career in national conservation.

In a broad way, every social interaction is a form of networking. If you think of job interviews (the subject of the next chapter) as both opportunities for work and as potential connections that may be useful even if you don't get the job, you will make the task of interviewing more pleasant and promising.

CHAPTER SEVEN

~

Ace Your Interviews

You miss 100 percent of the shots you don't take.

—Wayne Gretzky

Getting called in for an interview can feel like a major victory—and it is! It means your résumé was impressive enough to put you in the running. You're that much closer to getting the job you've sought.

Now all you have to do is confidently and concisely demonstrate that you would be the perfect candidate—exceptionally experienced and skilled, committed to the company, and a pleasure to work with, and all in just a few minutes. Is it any wonder that job interviews set off alarm bells for new grads?

An interview can be extremely stressful, and it can feel like your whole life depends on your performance. This anxiety may be enough to make you want to run in the other direction! The most important thing you can do in preparing for an interview is to remain calm, confident, and optimistic.

After all, you have every right to be confident. Remember, they are interviewing you because they need to hire someone—*they* need *you*. They've already seen how you look on paper, and what they saw interested them enough to make them want to talk with you. Whether multinationals or one-man shops, companies don't hire people out of sympathy or charity, and they don't interview people to do them a favor. You are not asking for a handout; you are offering them your abilities and experience, because you know that you will be good for their business and their bottom line. If they bring you in for an interview, they are already partway to agreeing with you.

Prior to an interview, think about what skills and understandings you have gained in previous jobs or experiences, as discussed in chapter 5. Another point stressed before that bears repeating: if asked about your last employer, never speak negatively. Even if you left that job because you hated everything about it, it is important that you still be able to explain how that work prepared you to be the best possible person for this job. Remember also that speaking negatively about anyone or any organization only reflects poorly on you. Stay positive.

Now let's enlarge on a point raised earlier in this book: In order to convey a sense of confidence effectively, you must know exactly what the company does and what its needs are. For instance, someone interviewing for a job as a camera operator at a production company would be wise to know what kind of projects this company normally does, the kind of clients with whom they usually work, and what kind of equipment they generally use. If your experience is in reality television, and this company makes videos for museums, you might still be the right person for the job, but it will be important that you can explain why your experience will help you meet their specific needs.

Researching the company also will prepare you for responding to questions an interviewer might put to you. Anticipating these questions allows you to prepare answers ahead of time, so you are not caught off-guard. Typical questions might include: What are your strengths? What are your weaknesses? Is there anything you don't like to do? Do you have an aversion to travel? What professional mistakes have you made in the past, and what did you learn from them?

The key question you should ask yourself as you prepare for an interview is this: How have my education, work experience, and personal abilities made me the perfect person for this job? Whether or not this is your dream job, you need to think in those terms in order to be able to explain clearly why your interviewer should hire you.

Go into each interview with enthusiasm and a smile. Dress well, sit up straight, and speak with confidence. It doesn't matter who else is applying for the job; all that matters is your ability to describe clearly and confidently who you are and why you're perfect for the position.

Aside from someone who shows up drunk and disheveled, few things are less attractive to a potential employer than someone who is not actually interested in the job. Ideally, any job for which you apply should be one that interests you. But maybe, with some jobs you apply for at the start of your career, all you care about is the paycheck and the insurance. Either way you need to be able to convince the interviewer that you specifically want *this* job and not just *a* job, which is why doing a little research on the company website can make a big difference in demonstrating your commitment.

Be prepared with a few specific questions to ask at the end of the interview. Asking questions is an important part of an interview, because your questions show an interest in your potential employer. Examples of questions might be these: How is the organization doing financially? What projects do they have coming up? What particular challenges do they see in the future? And if they hired you, what would your first day on the job entail? Are there opportunities for advancement?

> One time at an interview I foolishly lapsed into a mini-rant about my previous employer's unfair deadlines. I said something like, "They'd give me hours and hours of footage and then demand a rough cut in two days!" Not only did my petulance cast me in a negative light, but it made me look lazy—like I was just looking for an easy job with no challenges. Needless to say, they didn't hire me. —Alexander Gillies, grad student

Finally, be politically savvy during an interview, which means be smart enough to avoid discussing politics at all, and keep away from offering political opinions. You may have no idea what your interviewer thinks, and you might unintentionally offend him or her with your partisan views. You and the interviewer, and, later, others on staff if you get the job, are there to work together, not divide along political lines.

No matter how well you perform in an interview, you won't get hired every time. You might feel crushed if you don't get the job, but if you can confidently speak to your abilities and demonstrate a commitment to performing excellent work, you will ultimately find the job you're looking for. Think of job interviews as a way of honing your presentation skills—something that will be of value in the long run.

> In a recent job search, I got to the final round of interviews for one opening. I calmed my nerves and prepared relentlessly the week before. The interview went great, but I did not get the job. It was the first time I had ever been turned down for anything, and the experience made me question and doubt myself. But I made a decision to think on the positives, including the great experience of the process itself and what I learned from it. —Nick Zachar, grad student

CHAPTER EIGHT

~

Avoid the Worst Mistakes

Working hard and working smart sometimes can be two different things.

—Byron Dorgan

Searching for and finding a job is likely to be a laborious process. Whether you have been through several interviews in the recent past or your last interview was ten years ago, job seekers face numerous pitfalls. Here are seven mistakes you should avoid:

1. *Being late for an interview.* This admonition may seem like a no-brainer, but it is easy to leave the house a few minutes later than planned, get caught in traffic, or get turned around. When heading to an interview, always build in extra time—a half hour at least, even a full hour—for unexpected delays. Even if your appointment is scheduled for someplace you've been many times before, you never know what may come up, especially if you live in a large, traffic-jammed, urban area.

   Showing up punctually demonstrates respect for other people's time. If allowing extra time for travel gets you to an interview early, go to the address of your destination, then find a spot nearby where you can await the appointed time. Use the downtime to review notes about the company with which you are interviewing or to go over potential questions. And if, despite your best laid plans, you do find yourself running late, be sure to call your interviewer and let him or her know.

2. *Asking, "What does this company do?"* Hiring managers viscerally cringe when they hear questions like that. Do not go into an interview unprepared. Research the company, the position you are applying for, and the person who is interviewing you. If possible, have a point of contact with the company before you even apply. Connect with someone in the company through LinkedIn or in another professional way. Become familiar with the company's mission statement and ask well-thought-out questions the day of the interview.

As a senior in college, I was interviewing over the phone for a paid internship at the EPA. It lasted maybe fifteen to twenty minutes and went fairly well. At the end, the woman conducting the interview asked me if I had any questions. I was honestly exhausted and ready to get off the phone, but I felt that I should have some kind of follow-up. So I asked some fairly basic questions about the specific program I was applying for, some of which (and this is the part that kills me in retrospect) I already knew the answers to, just to have something to ask. I learned later that I essentially blew the whole interview in the last two minutes by asking these very basic questions that made it seem like I hadn't done any research about the job I was applying for. This was a tough learning experience for me, but now I know:

- Do your homework about the job you're applying for, and let the employer know that you've done this homework (without being excessive).
- Don't be afraid about not having any questions at the end of an interview.
- If you do have questions, ask intelligent ones.
- Don't let your game down at the very end of an interview. You can make or break it as you're walking out the door. —Sam Sheline, grad student

3. *Being unprepared to talk with people you meet.* In the process of searching for a job, you might find yourself at a few career or networking events. Prepare a concise "elevator speech" describing who you are and what your career goal is. Always have business cards and a couple of résumés handy. Although you might not walk out with a job, you are planting seeds for future meaningful relationships. Promptly follow up with any people with whom you've connected. When contacting them, do not directly ask for a job. Instead, thank them for their time, follow up with any specific information you learned at the meeting, and offer your help and knowledge to them.

4. *Assuming you're résumé is already at it's best.* Did you notice the grammatical errors in the previous phrase? A hiring manager probably would. Double-, triple-, and quadruple-check for spelling and punctuation errors. Do not rely solely on your word processor. Once you perfect your cover letter and résumé, have a colleague or adviser review them.

5. *Sending your résumé without an individualized approach.* Once you have found a position for which you are qualified, write a personalized cover letter and tailor your résumé. An incorrectly addressed cover letter or a long résumé with a list of non-applicable achievements will end up in the hiring manager's wastebasket. Remember that your cover letter is as important as your résumé, so make it warm, enthusiastic, and distinctive.

6. *Doing an interview without practicing your responses.* As noted earlier, whether you are entering the workforce for the first time or are a seasoned professional, interviews can be challenging. Reach out to career-counseling organizations. Many of these will conduct mock interviews with you. Practicing your responses aloud can make you aware of unnecessary repetition or ticks you may have, such as saying "like" or tapping your feet. Be ready for curveballs the interviewer might throw your way. Remember, your goal is to create a level of trust and real connection with the interviewer. Don't be passive—go with prepared points you want to make.

7. *Allowing embarrassing or compromising photos of yourself online.* I've said this already, but it's worth repeating. Be aware of the content you post on social-media sites. Employers often peruse candidates' pages. It is not only photographs that can dismay a potential employer, but negative comments about your current employer or anything that seems disrespectful or harebrained. On the same note, make sure to use a professional e-mail address on your résumé and business cards. Hiring managers might not share your sense of humor.

New college grads are leaving behind a place where certain attitudes and modes of dress earned them social points, and they are entering a world where those same modes of behavior can lead them to rejection from the workforce. In the highly competitive task of trying to land your first professional job, stack the deck in your favor. Meet the standards of deportment that are natural to your career milieu, and avoid the pitfalls outlined here that could leave you wondering why you are not even close to landing a dream job.

CHAPTER NINE

~

Think Outside the Box

Don't ask yourself what the world needs. Ask yourself what makes you come alive and go do that, because what the world needs is people who have come alive.

—Howard Thurman

Some of the most successful career paths are the least traditional. My own took many unexpected twists and turns. Some of the following may be familiar to you if you've read my book *Confessions of a Wildlife Filmmaker.*

In my late teens, not knowing what I wanted to do with my life, I meekly followed my father into naval ship design for the Royal Navy. My father's lifelong focus on warships and submarines had driven him from a working-class background in rural Wales to the top of his profession, and he won high recognition from the queen, who bestowed on him prestigious awards.

But the truth was that designing warships didn't interest me. Important as the work was, I wanted to devote my life to something more inspiring and less militaristic. I yearned to wake up each day with a sense of purpose. I longed to find an honorable cause that would do something to improve the world. My goal was to throw myself into a noble social movement, something far bigger than myself.

No great life event triggered my decision to dedicate my life to conservation and protecting the environment. There was no epiphany or revelation, just a gradual awakening fueled by books, lectures, articles, and films. Vivid images of polar bears, poignant footage of humpback whales singing, and inspirational words (such as Margaret Mead's "Never doubt that a small group of thoughtful, committed citizens can change the world; indeed, it's the only thing that ever has.") all spurred me to pursue this line of work. I felt the rightness of protecting the air, water, land, and animals from abuse and exploitation at the deepest part of my being. It was, I sensed, the right thing to do.

I realized with increasing clarity that if I devoted my life to warship design, I would never be fulfilled. So I left my work in engineering and searched for ways to break into environmental protection and energy conservation.

I left the British Navy, got an advanced degree from the Kennedy School of Government at Harvard, and then worked for the giant consulting firm Booz Allen, for a U.S. senator on Capitol Hill, and at the Environmental Protection Agency as a political appointee for President Jimmy Carter.

After Ronald Reagan defeated Jimmy Carter in 1980, I left the government (the new Republican administration replaced Carter operatives like me), and I joined the National Audubon Society as a senior lobbyist. After a year or two, I started looking for new ways to win converts to conservation and shape public opinion. I proposed to the National Audubon Society board of directors that we make a film for television on conservation, and they agreed. I knew nothing about television, so I was in way over my head with this idea.

My thought (which seemed novel at the time) was to invite celebrities to host prime-time, hard-hitting environmental documentaries about conservation policy issues. The point was to combine sugar and medicine. Conservation was important, but no one was going to come home from a hard day's work and plop down in front of the TV to watch educational programming. To get people to watch, the show had to be leavened with entertainment, hence the inclusion of celebrities and the importance of crafting compelling stories.

I already knew the power of celebrities to attract attention to the causes they cared about. When I worked on Capitol Hill in the 1970s, I had watched, fascinated, as the legendary actress Elizabeth Taylor arrived for an unannounced visit to the Senate Gallery and, in doing so, brought the work of the Senate to a complete halt as senators gawked at her in stunned admiration.

Soon after I began working on the film idea for Audubon, serendipity struck. I heard that media mogul Ted Turner was looking to form partnerships with environmental organizations to create programs for prime-time television. While other organizations scrambled to develop ideas, I was ready to go—I had been working on television ideas for months. I immediately contacted Turner's key staff. They liked my ideas, introduced me to Ted, and we were off and running.

Well, not quite. As I described in my 2010 book *Shooting in the Wild*, the biggest obstacles I had to surmount were those inside Audubon. I spent weeks pitching my proposal to colleagues and explaining how the organization would benefit from getting into the television business. But antipathy and animus to the proposed partnership between Audubon and Ted Turner stubbornly persisted. Audubon board members worried that I was inexperienced and naive. Three senior vice presidents, concerned that my ideas for television programs were distracting the organization from its historic focus on *Audubon* magazine, tried to get me fired.

Fortunately, Russell Peterson, then president of the National Audubon Society, rejected this advice, and Audubon formed a partnership with Ted Turner to produce for TBS Superstation and PBS the type of environmental and wildlife shows I had been advocating. In this way, we hoped to reach and influence the people who elected our lawmakers, thus bringing to Capitol Hill the type of legislators who would support conservation in the first place.

As my own story shows, you might end up at a completely different place from the one where you started. Remember to keep an open mind, but at the same time, don't drift along—review and revise your personal mission statement so that you remain aligned with your deepest values.

Some of my students also have found success following untraditional and unexpected paths:

Janetta Depeppa, recent grad student

Even though I graduated almost a year ago, answering the question often asked by relatives and friends, "What are you doing now?," remains extremely difficult. Despite my inability to answer this question due to its multifaceted answer, I am proud of what I've done since I received that final transcript.

It all started when I decided I would graduate a semester early from college. Although I think my parents believed this would allow me to apply for jobs without the competition of most of my peers graduating in May, I saw this extra time as an opportunity to go abroad and volunteer in a country I resolutely wanted to return to. So that's exactly what I did.

During my junior year, I studied abroad in South Africa, where I had the amazing opportunity to conduct independent research on South African economic development—a topic I could see myself pursuing as a career. I wanted more than anything to return to that beautiful, complicated country to continue this research and get a job there. Unfortunately, I soon found that visa laws had a different view in mind; it is extremely difficult to get a paid job as a foreigner, let alone as a foreigner with little formal work experience.

I approached my school's career adviser, telling him that I wanted to go back to South Africa, I wanted to work in my field of interest, and I wanted to do this immediately after graduation. His response was that I was being irrational. Rather than trying to find a job working in South Africa immediately after graduation, he said, I would be better suited taking a job in Washington, D.C., and working my way up through the company's ranks for a few years. His suggestion was that after a few years of working in D.C., I might have the opportunity to be transferred to South Africa.

This advice really upset me. Being a stereotypical twenty-something idealist, I wanted to impact my world, and I wanted to begin now. My passion was for South African economic development, and it didn't make sense that I had to pretend to want to do something else for the first few years of my working career. After all, I had already spent years waiting until I graduated to finally have an impact on the world!

I decided I would pursue this goal on my own. I took extra shifts working at a local restaurant to save money, and after many late-night Google searches and applications, I found an internship position in Cape Town, South Africa. After saving all my money for a few months, I took the plunge and headed abroad for six months, serving as an unpaid intern by day and on the weekends pursuing my own independent research. I even took a part-time job as a studio assistant at a nearby art gallery to earn some pocket change (to the grand sum of $26.95 per week!).

I have since returned to the States and, although I have little more clarity about what I'm doing next with my life, interning in South Africa did help me to recognize what I want to pursue for a long-term career. If I had taken that desk job in D.C. right after graduation, I never would have had the job responsibilities and work experiences that I had in South Africa. Most importantly, taking that internship helped me to see that this work was truly what I wanted to do. I gained a level of confidence and certainty that never would have been possible if I hadn't taken the risk of moving to a foreign country without a stable source of income.

The lesson? I've learned that life has a funny way of working itself out. You simply must become your own catalyst.

Urjita Sudula, recent grad student

If someone had told me when I started college that my first job would be in the finance industry at a bulge-bracket bank, I would have laughed. I entered college knowing that I wanted to go to law school and practice criminal law as a prosecutor.

But as the years progressed, my interests changed until I was a rising senior working in transaction services in New York City. I received a full-time offer from my summer internship, but I was far from certain whether the job was the one for me. I was an international studies major with a passion for diplomacy and economic development in emerging markets and was not sure where working at a major bank fit with my degree and interests. On the other hand, I knew that banking is a global industry and that the people I worked with were more often than not from a different country and background.

In the end, I decided to sign my offer letter and return to the job because of the connections I'd made, the wide range of skills I'd learned, and the promise of an amazing job opportunity. At the very least, I will come out of it knowing more than I did when I went in.

Nevertheless, my path since graduation has been far from clear. The finance industry is always changing, and the division that I knew as a summer analyst has gone through significant restructuring and will continue to do so. The uncertainty that I face has taught me much and reminds me that I am in the real world now. I am lucky enough to have a strong support network comprised of my family, friends, and work colleagues, ranging from my fellow analysts up to my manager.

I am still not sure where I see myself years down the line, but I am beginning to accept that it is okay not to know. So that is where I am today: working and loving my job, but with the knowledge that no door is closed to me.

Susie Vulpas, recent grad student

In the second semester of my senior year, I landed the internship of my dreams—a scholar intern at a prominent think tank focusing on science and technology in society and politics.

During this time, I began my application for the Peace Corps, something in which I had always wanted to participate. But after I graduated, my internship was promoted from part time to full time, and when the lowest-level staff member on the project left the team, I had aspirations of attaining her role. Days, weeks, and months went by, and, despite my attempts, the role remained vacant, and I stayed an intern.

Ten months after I had started my internship, I was offered a position with the Peace Corps. Even though I had a full-time, paid internship that might eventually have led to that low-level position, I decided to walk headfirst into this nerve-racking adventure and spend the next twenty-seven months as a Peace Corps volunteer in Mali. I figured there was no better first experience out of college than one that traded a cubicle for a mud hut in rural Africa.

Reflecting back on that decision now, I'm sure I would have found success at that think tank, but I also would have held myself back from the amazing, eye-opening experience I had in Mali. My philosophy today, as it was then, is to venture and live without regrets!

~

PART III

MAXIMIZE YOUR PRODUCTIVITY

Days are expensive. When you spend a day, you have one less day to spend. So make sure you spend each one wisely.

—Jim Rohn

How do I manage my time? How can I stop wasting so much time? I have dozens of to-do lists, but is that effective? How can I stop being overwhelmed by e-mail? I feel stressed and constantly fatigued—what can I do?

~

CHAPTER TEN

Manage Your Time Effectively

Don't judge each day by the harvest you reap, but by the seeds you plant.

—Robert Louis Stevenson

Successful professionals tend to manage their time effectively and thus lead highly productive lives. They know what they want to achieve, and they manage their time and organize their schedules accordingly. They don't waste time on meaningless television programs, mindless gossip, or other counterproductive activities unrelated to their chief goals. And they don't procrastinate—they have a plan, and they stick to it.

I'm a terrible procrastinator. A friend and I worked for years on a screenplay—a political satire—that we both loved. We loved it so much that we kept putting it off, thinking, *This could be great, so we don't want to mess it up. Let's wait until we can spend the time to make it really good.* Little did we realize that politics change and, before you know it, your political satire is a historical relic. The window for following through on good ideas can be pretty slim sometimes— don't procrastinate! —Alexander Gillies, grad student

Here are nine steps you can take to manage your time better:

1. *Focus on what matters most to you in your professional and personal life.* You'll make the most rapid gains in productivity when you cease to pursue jobs, contracts, careers, or relationships that you find trivial or that don't really relate to your passions or your work. Your goal is to achieve congruence between how you spend your day and what matters most to you. Again, referring back to your personal mission statement can help you to keep your eyes on the big picture.

> As I started in graduate school, I began to realize that in order to take the time I needed to succeed academically, I needed to give up some of my other opportunities. I evaluated what activities in my schedule could be forfeited to reduce my stress and improve my academic goals. I then approached my professional contacts and respectfully terminated my positions with them. Although initially I felt bad about leaving these positions, I realized that it is okay to say no if that means you can manage your life more effectively. I made sure I left on positive terms and maintained contact with individuals for the future. —Shannon Lawrence, grad student

2. *Set long-term goals for what you want to accomplish and break them down into more manageable short-term goals.* Knowing your long-term goals— and the short-term steps you need to take to get there—will vastly improve your ability to use your time effectively. This enhancement is true not just for work, but also for your personal life. Spending time with family and friends and pursuing fulfilling and rewarding hobbies is essential for living a happy, balanced life. Just as with work, you want to get the most out of that time.
3. *Plan weekly, not daily.* Planning daily is problematic because it is too easy to get caught up in the minutiae of urgent activities and to lose the connection between your commitments (your important strategic goals) and the daily rush of meetings, phone calls, e-mail, and so forth. Have a regular time once a week (I do it on Sunday evening) when you review your personal mission statement and your commitments. Block time on your calendar for these activities.

    In this way, you put the "big rocks" on your calendar first so they don't get squeezed out by the unimportant "pebbles." For example, if one of your commitments is "to repair a strained relationship with a colleague," then at the start of the week schedule time (perhaps lunch) with that person. In this way, you can begin to spend more time on those relationships, projects, and goals that matter most to you.

4. *Make sure your actions pass the SMART test: Specific, Measurable, Attainable, Realistic, and Time-sensitive.* For example, if one of your long-range goals is to write a book on your family history, then a few of the shorter-term commitments could be: interview your mom and dad by June 1, find a genealogy coach who can help you by July 1, find all the photos in your parents' home relating to your grandparents and their parents by August 1, and so on.

5. *Put your goals in writing.* Without written goals, your life is essentially drifting without focus. Goals turn your hopes into plans, and plans turn your dreams into reality.

6. *After you've set your goals and made plans to achieve them, get to work.* Don't start each day in the office by surfing the Internet, searching YouTube, or checking in on Facebook unless those activities involve a specific professional goal. Starting the day by mounting the digital surfboard can drown you in wasted time. Instead, select the most important and valuable strategic task you are facing and work on that until it is finished. Tackling your biggest challenge first will set you up to storm through the rest of your day brimming with self-confidence and enthusiasm. This practice also will help you avoid the trap of procrastination.

7. *Keep a to-do list.* Whenever you take on a new task, don't store it in your head, which will only clutter your mind unnecessarily. Instead, add it to your to-do list. Freeing your mind for the task at hand will sharpen your thinking and increase your effectiveness and productivity.

8. *Cross off items one by one as you finish them.* This practice will keep track of your progress and motivate you to keep going. If you finish a task that, for some reason, is not on your list, put it on the list anyway and immediately cross it out. At the end of the day, when you review your accomplishments, you will then have a complete—and encouraging—report of what you've done.

9. *Focus on things that are important rather than urgent.* Urgent unimportant tasks that come up throughout the day can easily cause you to veer offtrack from your most important goals. Keep in mind that unimportant but urgent matters (e.g., interruptions, gossip, some meetings and phone calls, and other people's minor issues) should rarely be given priority over important yet not necessarily urgent matters (e.g., getting feedback, building relationships, planning, preparation, reflection, learning, personal development, and seizing new opportunities). It can

In college, I would waste time on meaningless things (at least meaningless now that I look back on them). For example, I would watch way too much TV. When I got stressed over exams, and so forth, I would de-stress by watching TV. This actually led me to being even more stressed. I have learned that to de-stress it is important to do the little things every day so you can stay caught up on life. Now the time I used to spend on TV, I invest in daily tasks or in reading books that add to my knowledge, making me feel more accomplished at the end of the day. —Nick Zachar, grad student

be helpful to remind yourself of what is important as opposed to urgent by reviewing your to-do list each morning and reminding yourself of your priorities for the day's and the week's work.

Time management is at heart the management of your life. Each week, day, and hour that passes is one less chance to achieve, to excel, to dream, to do. It goes without saying that time is our most-precious commodity. Managing time correctly shows personal respect for your goals and for yourself.

~

CHAPTER ELEVEN

Make Your To-Do List Work for You

The secret of a person's success is discovered in their daily agenda.

—John C. Maxwell

The last chapter mentioned to-do lists as a way to manage your time more effectively.

Perhaps, at the end of the workday, you arrive home from school or the office exhausted, struggling to recall one thing you accomplished that day. You may feel dissatisfied because you don't seem to have made any progress on your projects. You may become convinced that your day has been wasted despite the frenetic rush of meetings, phone calls, and e-mails. But if you were to take control of your routine via a daily to-do list, you would soon find that the end of each workday leaves you feeling fulfilled and satisfied.

Follow these nine steps to make your to-do list work for you:

1. Derive your to-do list as much as possible from your personal mission statement so that every day you are moving your life forward in the direction you want to go, not simply reacting to someone else's agenda. Set aside one time a week to come up with goals for the week ahead.

2. Write down your to-do list first thing in the morning before distractions begin (or before you go to bed the night before). Don't rely on a mental list. Check this list against your weekly goals. Are there any tasks that can be delegated or deleted?

3. Make your desired outcomes specific. Instead of "Contract for Barnes," write, "Review contract for Barnes, especially the deliverables, and then send it to Fred in HR." Start each item on your to-do list with an action verb.

4. Have only one list for the day ahead. Consolidate all lists into one master list, either on paper or electronically. Break down big jobs into smaller ones.

5. Capture *all* of your tasks for the day and put them on your to-do list. This practice gives you a comprehensive list that includes everything you need to accomplish. Add any new task to the master list. Don't use sticky notes or pieces of scrap paper. If a new task takes less than two minutes, do it immediately without adding it to the list.

6. As I've mentioned before, when you complete a task, put a check beside it or draw a line through it. You'll feel a satisfying sense of accomplishment that will improve your mood and motivate you to keep going.

7. Put your list of to-dos in order of importance. You can work effectively on only one task at a time. Work on the first task until it's complete, and then move on to no. 2. This approach allows you to work with total concentration on the task at hand without worrying that you might be forgetting to do something important.

8. Focus on what is important, not what is urgent. Again, as discussed in the previous chapter, don't let urgent but unimportant tasks take all of your attention, leading you down a rabbit hole of follow-up activities so deep that you lose sight of the bigger picture. Don't procrastinate; take care of the important tasks that are critical to your professional success, even though they are not urgent.

9. As the day progresses, keep asking yourself, *Of all the items remaining on my to-do list, which one is the most important right now?* The answer to that question constitutes the best use of your time. Reorder your priorities as appropriate.

Adhering to this process will boost your productivity, help you make steady progress toward your most important goals, and allow you to arrive home from the office feeling less anxious and more fulfilled.

CHAPTER TWELVE

~

Use E-Mail Effectively and Efficiently

We become what we think about.

—Earl Nightingale

With so much work conducted virtually, it is important to use e-mail effectively and efficiently. Here are suggestions for how to manage your e-mails successfully:

- At the start of each day, I personally like to check my e-mail and deal with it quickly. I am most relaxed when I have only one or two e-mails in my inbox.
- Some people think that keeping e-mail open constantly while you work prevents you from focusing on important tasks. They recommend allocating certain hours to read and respond to e-mails. Personally, I like to keep my e-mail on as I work so that I can respond quickly when appropriate. In this way, I keep a few short responses from accumulating into a massive task that would interrupt my schedule if all responses had to be done at one time later in the day. Whether you choose to leave your e-mail on while you work will depend on the needs of your job and your personal preference.
- If you find yourself on e-mail—or Facebook or YouTube—when you weren't planning to be, make a conscious decision to close it and return to your work. Refer to your to-do list or plan for the day to recall what you should be doing.

I like the idea of turning off e-mails during certain hours. I might even take it a step further! Sometimes I turn off my phone or retreat from my computer. Facebook and text messages are a tremendous drain on precious time—especially for people from my generation. —Will Reid, grad student

- When you do attend to your e-mails, be focused! To the greatest extent possible, respond immediately once you read an e-mail so it is dealt with and done. Respond in a clear and succinct manner, and don't ramble. Your goal is to respond so effectively that you end the exchange of e-mails.
- If you aren't able to respond fully to a significant e-mail, send a quick message acknowledging it so the sender knows you have received it and isn't left wondering what's happened to it. If you are not the right person to answer a particular question, direct the sender to someone who is.
- Delete all unimportant e-mails and those you have dealt with. Clear your inbox within eight hours or sooner. Keep e-mails in your inbox only as a reminder of something important to you. File or archive messages that you might need in the future.
- Include your telephone number on all e-mails so people can easily contact you if they need to.
- Remember that every e-mail represents who you are to the working world. It is important that your e-mails be free of typos, misspelling, grammatical errors, and other mistakes. Always use spell-check and reread your message before pushing the "Send" button.
- Use clear, informal, and personal language. Don't use exclamation points in professional e-mails, and avoid the passive voice. It is clearer to write "Fred has made a film about toxics" than "A film has been made by Fred about toxics." Don't write in all capital letters. It looks like you're yelling.
- Always be courteous. Don't write an e-mail in anger. Calm down and then, if at all possible, talk to the person with whom you're angry. If you cannot talk, try not to be negative or express your anger in the e-mail. It's likely to come back to haunt you.
- Use a subject line that clearly states what your e-mail is about. If you reply to a message on one topic, but write on another topic, change your outgoing subject line to match the new topic.

- Cover one topic per e-mail. If that isn't possible, let the reader know the e-mail contains more than one topic by making the subject line "Four issues to discuss."
- Use "Bcc" when sending an e-mail to a large number of people. Put your own name in the "To" box. Your recipients don't want their e-mail addresses sent to strangers.
- When saying thank you for something, don't copy everyone on the e-mail, just the person you're thanking.

E-mail is one of the greatest tools of the digital age. It's easy to use, saves paper, allows you to contact people without creating the potential interruption of a phone call and allows them to respond when doing so fits their schedules, and produces a written record of your correspondence—something a phone call does not do. But it can also turn into a great time consumer if you do not approach it with awareness of what you are trying to accomplish. The few simple rules outlined here should help you make e-mail a powerful tool in your professional repertoire.

CHAPTER THIRTEEN

∼

Manage and Reduce Stress

Obstacles are those frightful things you see when you take your eyes off your goals.

—Hannah More

To have some stress in your life is natural. In fact, a certain level of stress is good. You want to feel challenged and alive. You want to strive for excellence. But sometimes stress can leave you despondent, enervated, and even apathetic—feelings that drastically reduce your effectiveness.

In order to combat stress, you must take care of yourself physically, socially, emotionally, mentally, spiritually, and financially. In this chapter, and throughout the book, you will find useful practices for a balanced and healthy life, but keep in mind that people can have different rhythms and habits and still be healthy. The key is to be aware of your choices and make sure that they truly work for you. Here are some general measures you can take to reduce stress. Fitness will be discussed in more detail in the next chapter.

- You can take on daily challenges only if you are *physically healthy*. Exercising regularly, getting enough sleep, and eating a healthy and balanced diet are all ways that help keep your body ready to meet those challenges. Studies show that rigorous exercise for an hour every day, including flexibility, strength, and cardio exercises, will keep you in good form.

In high school I was a pretty good athlete and in really good shape. I worked out twice daily for the sports I was involved in (football, wrestling, track). Once I got to college, I didn't have the motivation of sports to push me to work out every day. I stopped exercising, gained weight, and felt more and more sluggish. Finally I had had enough. I set goals such as losing weight or trying a new workout. I decided to go to bed one hour earlier and wake up one hour earlier so I could go for a jog or go to the gym at school. I became healthier not only physically but also mentally and emotionally. I also noticed that my drive for success increased. —Nick Zachar, grad student

- Your *social and emotional well-being* will give you the strength and confidence to overcome stressful setbacks. Maintaining healthy friendships and learning how to be a loving and generous friend and partner are all ways to ensure that relationships with loved ones will de-stress rather than stress you.
- Taking care of your *mental and spiritual health* will eliminate some of the typical causes of stress and provide you a foundation upon which you can grow. As mentioned earlier, keys to such health include ridding your life of duplicity and living according to your values. Being honest with yourself and others and behaving in a way that matches your values will allow you to lead a life that is characterized by personal fulfillment and high productivity.
- Finally, take care of your *finances* as best you can. Credit-card debt can be crippling. Get help from one of the many books or online services that cover financial management.

With a baseline of physical, social, emotional, mental, spiritual, and financial health, you are in a much better position to manage any stressful situation that arises.

When you are feeling stressed, pinpoint the specific causes. If, for example, you know that your job is the cause of the stress, dig a little deeper and ask yourself what exactly about the job is causing it. Is it the amount of work? Is it your relationships with bosses and coworkers? Do you feel stressed because the work is unfulfilling?

After pinpointing the cause of stress, think about what actions you can take to mitigate it or to change the conditions that cause it. You should deal with the problem as soon as possible to avoid harboring negative feelings that hurt both your work and personal life. For example, you could talk with

> Right after getting my undergrad film degree, I started a wedding videography company. I actually have little to no interest in wedding videography, but, despite my gut feeling, I rationalized it by telling myself, "Hey, I've got to start somewhere."
>
> The entire time I ran my company, I dreaded going to work. I was stressed and listless—and as a result, my company went nowhere. The truth is, I'd have been happier working as the lowest-paid production assistant on a film set than as owner of a wedding-videography company. I came to realize this only years later, when I met people who were passionate about wedding videography (a species I previously hadn't thought existed), and it clicked for me—there are no "starter" jobs and "goal" jobs; there are only jobs you care about and jobs you don't. —Alexander Gillies, grad student

your boss about your workload or invite to lunch a coworker with whom you haven't gotten along.

What if you feel stress because your current job is not fulfilling to you? When you spend hours of every workday in a field for which you have no passion, it's easy to feel resentful, harassed, and anxious. Of course, in this situation, you might consider finding a different job, but doing so is, far too often, very difficult, especially at the start of a career. So, consider looking at your current job, however unfulfilling, as just the first step down a pathway that will help take you to your long-term goals. Why are you there instead of in your dream job? Is it because you need more experience, a stronger background, better credentials? Your current job may be the vehicle to all those intermediate objectives.

Meanwhile, try to find fulfillment in this job the best you can. Find mentors and ask for more responsibilities. Be a consummate perfectionist in everything you do. Smile, be helpful, and do the tasks that everyone else hates. Remember that you are working toward your goals—that knowledge, in itself, should help reduce your stress. Your present situation won't last forever.

> I have an entry-level position, so though I am learning a lot, there aren't many opportunities to create things of value, to feel like I'm really helping to better the world. I realize this is typical of my position. So I am trying to learn as much as possible to move forward in my career and hopefully reach a point soon where I'm doing more meaningful work. In the meantime, I am trying to create a meaningful life outside of work. I have begun to teach myself Photoshop and InDesign, skills that I believe can be beneficial to my career. I journal daily. I read as much as possible. Anything to make myself grow and, therefore, feel fulfilled. —Recent grad student

CHAPTER FOURTEEN

~

Increase Your Vitality

Healthy citizens are the greatest asset any country can have.

—Winston S. Churchill

Most Americans struggle with some degree of fatigue, lethargy, and irritability. But success at work—and at *finding* work—depends on being physically, mentally, and emotionally vibrant. Our minds should be sharp, alert, and focused throughout the day so that we complete our tasks effectively and accomplish our goals.

Here are some tips that can help:

- *Establish a morning routine that wakes you up.* This might include making breakfast, doing yoga, meditating, going for a run, or slowly drinking your coffee.
- *Exercise.* We all know exercise is good for our health, but it can also boost our creativity, increase our energy levels, and lift our moods. Start the day with exercises that will wake up your body and mind.

In the mornings, before checking my e-mail or taking on any other task, I kick-start my brain by sitting down with a cup of coffee and reading some famously difficult novel. I've come to terms with the fact that I don't really get postmodernism, but I've found that reading a few pages from a David Foster Wallace novel can really get the juices flowing—even if only in confused frustration. —Alexander Gillies, grad student

Even a short, simple stretching routine can help. A neighborhood stroll, or biking to work, can kick-start your day, giving you instant energy and long-term fitness. Working out with weights, and focusing on body movement as you do so, can be relaxing and even meditative, both building strength and removing you restfully from the day's stresses. Stretching on your own or in a class also is relaxing and will help you prevent injuries from overextension.

- *Keep moving throughout the day.* If you experience drowsiness after lunch, try walking briskly for a few minutes and stretching. If you are at your desk and feel your energy slipping away, take a few seconds to get up and stretch or do a few jumping jacks. If you're in a meeting with a colleague and notice the energy in the room waning, suggest that you continue the meeting while standing up, or outside in the fresh air, or strolling through the hallways. Some fitness experts recommend getting up from your desk and computer keyboard for at least five minutes of every hour to improve and maintain healthy circulation.
- *Eat a nutritious breakfast.* Don't grab a doughnut and coffee as you rush out the door and jump into your car. If you find yourself skipping breakfast due to a lack of time, keep healthy food ready to go. For example, you could quickly eat some oatmeal or a low-sugar, high-fiber cereal, or even just grab some fruit and nuts or a yogurt. A whole-grain bagel, low in fat, is a good substitute for a doughnut or pastry if you must eat while driving to work.
- *Continue to eat healthily throughout the day.* If you find yourself rushing from one meeting to the next, grabbing a cookie or other unhealthy snack to tide you over, try planning ahead—keep healthy snacks such as nuts, carrots, and raisins at the office. An apple a day helps lower cholesterol levels in the blood, and apples, which come in a wide range of flavors and tastes, are easy to keep at work.
- *Sleep well, and sleep enough.* If you hit the snooze button on your alarm clock several times and still have to drag yourself out of bed, you might

I once came to Professor Palmer for his thoughts on diet, and he recommended some resources. I was not eating the best, and I could tell this was leading to negative impacts on my health, mentally and physically. I remember taking certain foods out of my diet one at a time (first soda, then milk, then red meat, and so forth) usually at week intervals. I would substitute each one with a new, healthy alternative. Since then I have completely reshaped my diet, lost significant weight, and I feel healthier and more energetic each day. —Nick Zachar, grad student not be getting enough sleep. A good night's rest brings clarity, energy, and a good mood. Several studies have revealed that getting only six hours of sleep each night for three nights in a row will impair your mental acuity as much as if you were inebriated. When you do have a sleep deficit, you may need several nights of long sleep to recover.

Make it a routine to go to sleep and wake up at roughly the same time each day, allowing your mind and body to become accustomed to a regular activity pattern. Make sure you sleep enough each night, whether you personally need seven hours or ten. Make your sleeping environment conducive to a good night's rest. Turn off your cell phone, tablet, computer, and other electronics—the blue light given off by electronics counters your body's production of melatonin, which is needed for sleep. Cut off social websites and Internet surfing at least twenty minutes before bedtime—this downtime will tell your brain that it is time to rest and make it easier for you to fall asleep. The lights cast by television screens, particularly the bright bursts typical of many shows and commercials, stimulate the brain and can keep it from slipping into a more peaceful state.

- *Exercise your brain.* Sometimes we think that only our muscles need activity, but our brain is a powerful organ that needs to be kept stimulated, too. Try memorizing a few phone numbers instead of immediately reaching for your phone's contact list. Mentally tally your purchases at the store, challenge yourself with a crossword puzzle, or make it a point to recall the names of everyone you've met throughout the day. Plenty of online games, such as Lumosity.com, can challenge your mind. If you have children, a memory-card game or flashcards are fun.
- *Learn something new.* You might not have time to learn a new language or instrument, but keep trying new things, such as a new recipe. Or you might pick up chess, listen to a radio station in a different language, learn new words, or learn the lyrics to songs you hear on the car radio. The brain craves information, and the more you challenge it, the more it will gain strength and power. To put it another way: Venture outside your comfort zone. My father learned Spanish in his spare time in his sixties.

Finally, at the end of the day, when you are in bed preparing to doze off, consider a simple exercise that may brighten your dreams and allow you to wake in a positive mood. Ask yourself to list three good things that happened to you that day. Too often, we fail to notice the good things, and we dwell on the bad or the disappointing. Ending each day with thoughts about successes or achievements, kindnesses or affections, will bolster positive thoughts and a sense that each day gives you something to be happy about.

CHAPTER FIFTEEN

~

Boost Your Productivity Even More

Create the kind of self that you will be happy to live with all your life. Make the most of yourself by fanning the tiny, inner sparks of possibility into flames of achievement.

—Golda Meir

To achieve your goals, you need the involvement of other people. Consequently, your success in interacting with people will likely be reflected in your success as a professional. Here are ten keys to boosting your own productivity by leveraging your contacts.

1. *Listen attentively and actively to other people.* Taking the time to listen shows that you respect the people with whom you interact, which in turn strengthens your relationships with them. They are more likely to give you the same kind of respectful attention. And you both are more likely to understand what the other person is attempting to convey, which will help you to avoid costly mistakes and wasted time.

2. *Take your commitments, however small, very seriously.* When you promise to do something, do it—and do it when you say you will, if not sooner.

3. *Move quickly, and develop a reputation for speed and reliability.* Take important phone calls immediately. As already mentioned, complete all small jobs (under a couple of minutes) right away. Respond quickly to requests from people with whom you have important relationships (your spouse, your boss, your children, and so on).

I frequently find myself saying yes to requests, which often lands me in a nonstop work cycle—or a nonstop cycle of social obligations. It is absolutely crucial to be true to your own goals and not let your time be sidetracked by the expectations or desires of others. This, of course, does not mean that we cannot be generous or helpful with others. But it is important to be aware of our commitments and to sign on only for those things that we have the time and space for. —Will Reid, grad student

4. *Be comfortable saying no and declining requests from others.* At a low-level job, you might not feel as if you always have the option to say no. But whenever possible, take on only tasks and projects that are important for your long-term goals.

5. *Establish routines.* Some people find that they lack the self-discipline to carry out their to-do lists or even to create them in the first place. If you have this problem, establish a routine so that the tasks become second nature. For instance, you might set aside a particular time every day to exercise or a particular time every week to write down your goals for that week.

6. *Break your big, challenging projects into smaller, more manageable pieces.* Though mentioned before, this practice is worth repeating, because large projects will arise again and again during your professional life. Long-term projects are intimidating, and it's easy to feel overwhelmed as you are starting out. Sometimes it's even easy to feel overwhelmed in the middle of a long project, when you know how much work you have already put in, while still seeing all the work that's left to do. Breaking down your projects into manageable tasks will help you stay engaged and focused on the task at hand.

7. *Avoid gossip.* It is important to spend time building good relationships with coworkers, but don't engage in office gossip or politics. Gossip

In my undergrad research project, I had a huge portion left to do with only months left until graduation. The task was extremely tedious. I had to crack open hundreds of little snails and measure their sizes under a microscope. I also had to analyze an enormous amount of data. I procrastinated, making the situation even worse. I consulted my mentor and let her know that I was overwhelmed. We broke down weekly tasks up to the deadline for my thesis. This approach took tons of pressure off of me, and each task was more of a mini-exercise rather than a huge, daunting project. So, seek advice from someone who will understand and help. Develop a plan. Execute the plan. —Nick Zachar, grad student may seem urgent, but it is always unimportant. If you get caught up in one of these conversations, politely withdraw and get back to your important tasks. Most people will recognize the choice you are making and respect you for it.

8. *To the extent possible, rid your life of other time-wasters, such as long commutes and poorly run meetings.* If you do have to attend a poorly run meeting, be on time and keep your input brief and to the point. Long commutes can be turned into productive periods if you travel by mass transit and apply the time to reading useful material, going over plans, or doing paperwork.

9. *Organize your workspace.* People who claim they work better from a messy desk are deluding themselves. Don't let your desk get covered with unorganized piles of paper. Handle each piece of paper once. Toss it, refer it to someone else, take action on it, or file it. When in doubt, throw it out.

I used to have a romantic idea of myself as the mechanic from *Zen and the Art of Motorcycle Maintenance* whose shop is a mess, but he knows exactly where everything is. Or so I felt, until I realized that I was so disorganized that I couldn't find my passport and, as a result, missed out on a cruise. Turns out that the passport was in exactly the spot I thought it was. I couldn't find it because of all the rest of the clutter. Trust me—you may be able to function with a messy desk, but it never helps. And sometimes it makes you miss a Disney cruise. —Alexander Gillies, grad student

10. *Take care of yourself.* As I've emphasized before, your physical, social/emotional, mental, and spiritual well-being are vital to the process of making you a more effective and fulfilled person.

Increased productivity is a worthwhile and persistent goal. But don't lose sight of the possibility that downtime also can be a form of productivity. Your mind and body may tire if you stick to one task too long. If you feel yourself flagging while working on a long-term project, consider switching to another task. Sometimes the best vacation is finding different work to do.

Research increasingly shows that while you sleep, the mind continues to work on problems that may have eluded you during the day. Motor skills, such as playing a musical instrument, seem to improve after a night's sleep, as does the ability to remember lists of items. If you begin to feel that you can't find the solution to a particular problem, try sleeping on it. When you wake in the morning, the solution may be the first thought that occurs to you. Know when to keep at it, and know when to rest.

PART IV

~

COMMUNICATE EFFECTIVELY

You will either step forward into growth or you will step back into safety.

—Abraham Maslow

How can I be an effective leader? What do I do if I'm in charge of running a meeting? How can I be strong and assertive without being rude? How can I become a powerful speaker and skilled panel moderator?

CHAPTER SIXTEEN

~

Be an Effective Leader

If you want to lift yourself up, lift up someone else.

—Booker T. Washington

Effective leadership involves many skills, and they are all learnable. Indeed, in reading the previous chapters, you already may have begun to learn some of these skills. Here are seven key elements of effective leadership that you should practice and attempt to master:

1. *Effective leaders take action.* They relentlessly instigate fresh initiatives. They constantly ask themselves, *What projects am I working on and what actions have I taken that can give rise to new goals and projects? What is the best use of my time right now, and what do I need to focus on?* Then they discipline themselves to focus on taking needed action.
2. *Effective leaders stay focused on their goals.* Leadership requires purposeful, goal-oriented activity. Your important strategic goals can get pushed out of the way quickly by the daily grind of meetings, e-mails, and phone calls. Don't let that happen.
3. *Effective leaders are willing to say no.* They are not afraid to say no to requests from colleagues and friends. Leaders don't allow their time to be whittled away by unimportant or tangential issues. They apply their energy to tasks and objectives that advance their own projects and agendas. They decline requests that don't.

I think for many of us, myself included, the temptation is always to say yes when asked for help. After all, yes is a pleasant word, and we want to please people! However, I have worked in firms where my boss said yes to many outside requests, spreading himself and the organization too thin. This approach can be unfair to the employees, as we are left looking like the bad guys when our boss made promises that were not possible for us to keep. —Will Reid, grad student

4. *Effective leaders are extraordinarily reliable.* They follow through on requests to which they *do* agree. A big reason to say no from time to time is to enable you to say yes to assignments and requests that help to fulfill your goals. We all know folks who agree to do something but end up dropping the ball. We've all made that mistake at some point—everyone's human. But a characteristic of effective leaders is this: If they say they're going to do something, they *do it*; if they make a promise, they *keep it*. Reliability and trustworthiness are key traits of successful leaders. Remember, life is a team sport—people are relying on you to achieve *your* goals so they can accomplish *theirs*, and you want to be a most-valued player.

5. *Effective leaders plan ahead.* They think big and boldly. This kind of thought requires planning. Meticulously review your goals and mission to make sure you're ready to tackle them. Plan for your week, month, and year instead of just the day ahead. It will be easier to commit to the bigger challenges if you block out the time they require. Put your big commitments on your calendar before it gets filled up with items from other people's agendas.

6. *Effective leaders listen.* They make a distinction between *hearing* and *listening.* It's easy to hear what someone says and generate a reply, but listening so that you deeply understand another person's frame of reference requires profound empathy. You don't have to agree with what people are saying, but you'll be a better leader if you make every effort to comprehend deeply a person's words and body language. As mentioned in a previous chapter, when you satisfy another person's need to be understood, the effort is more likely to be reciprocated. Clear and precise communication is essential to your own success and to the success of those you lead.

7. *Effective leaders are dedicated to self-improvement and lifelong learning.* They constantly look for opportunities to grow professionally and personally. They eschew stagnancy and lethargy. They are not afraid to reach out to friends and colleagues to request feedback and coaching.

Being an effective leader is not a solitary business. Jack Welch, former CEO of General Electric, said, "Before you are a leader, success is all about growing yourself. When you become a leader, success is all about growing others."

~

CHAPTER SEVENTEEN

Run Your Meetings Effectively

Progress and motion are not synonymous.

—Tim Fargo

There's nothing worse than a pointless meeting that drags on and on and accomplishes nothing. Don't let this happen when you are in charge. Here are some tips for running a meeting effectively:

1. The first question you should ask when planning a meeting is: What are the goals of this gathering? Ideally, the organization should have a general goal that everyone can contribute toward, as well as specific goals for individuals. By identifying the goals of the meeting beforehand, you can shape and direct the meeting to maximize its effectiveness.

2. Avoid trying to cram too many goals into one meeting; a meeting with an overstuffed agenda can turn into a confusing, directionless, and overly long morass from which everyone leaves feeling frustrated and lost. Conversely, make sure that the meeting *has* a definite goal. If there isn't a real purpose for the meeting, don't waste everyone's time. Consider whether you can learn what you need to know by making a quick phone call or sending a short e-mail rather than scheduling a meeting.

3. Once you have outlined the goals of the meeting, communicate them to everyone involved and give them the chance to prepare. Be sure to let everyone know what the meeting will cover and what level of

contribution is expected from the attendees. The more everyone can prepare, the more they can contribute, and the more value everyone will get from the meeting. As with all things in business and in life, good communication is essential.

4. Once you're in the meeting, it is important that you lead and direct it but that you also allow people in the room to contribute. When a meeting gets bogged down in minutiae and tangential conversation, it is often because the person leading it either did not come in with a clear plan or is not keeping things on point. Don't let this happen to you. Come in with a planned outline for the meeting, don't let things get too far off topic, and don't spend too much time on any one issue.

   At the same time, however, it is essential that you give your colleagues a chance to contribute and voice their opinions and concerns. Not only will this practice keep them involved and interested in the meeting, but it is likely that they will offer something valuable. Many bosses fall into the trap of thinking of meetings as a chance for them to lecture their employees. This tactic shows a remarkable lack of appreciation for the intelligence and insight that employees can offer. The employees will notice that lack of appreciation, zone out of the meeting, and feel generally less valued at the company.

5. Ask for ideas whenever appropriate. When working on a specific problem, you should ask participants to offer their ideas for solutions or for facets of the problem that need to be addressed. Write down their ideas on a screen or large pad where everyone can see them. This approach invests everyone in the process of the meeting and its outcome. When ideas slow down or halt, mark a large X at the bottom of the list to show that more ideas may be added later if they arise in someone's mind during or after the meeting. Brainstorming should be open ended.

6. Don't allow particularly aggressive attendees to dominate the discussion. Some people love to hear themselves talk, and their loquaciousness will keep others from contributing to the discussion or brainstorming session. However, everyone has to pause for a breath now and then. If someone is running on, watch for that moment when they take a breath, then cut in, thanking them for their participation and asking others if they have follow-up ideas.

7. Encourage people who do not actively participate in meetings to do so. Some people are simply too shy to talk during meetings, but they may be restraining very good ideas. Don't presume that their silence means they've nothing to say or add. During a meeting, watch participants' body language. If you sense someone is holding back, invite him or her

to speak. However, if you know someone is particularly reticent about speaking in a group, stop that person after the meeting and ask what he or she thought of the discussion and its conclusions. Some very bright people work more effectively one on one rather than in a group.

8. Create an action plan. At the end of a meeting, review any commitments you or other participants made. Be specific, such as, "You said you will have document X ready by next Wednesday, and meanwhile I will meet with my boss by tomorrow to discuss what we have determined to do at this meeting. We will meet again on such and such a date." In short, be sure everyone leaves with an agenda to accomplish before the next meeting on the same subject.

Meetings should zero in on an agenda, but don't try to squelch all friendly chatter. Meetings are also opportunities for employees who may rarely interact with one another to create bonds through humor and personal discussion, in effect addressing the larger agenda of creating a team. The trick is to avoid letting light, diversionary discussions outweigh a meeting's stated agenda.

CHAPTER EIGHTEEN

~

Foster Civility and Courtesy in the Workplace

I speak to everyone in the same way, whether he is the garbage man or the president of the university.

—Albert Einstein

We spend a great deal of our lives at work. An atmosphere of civility and courtesy in the workplace is often key to whether you enjoy or dread your job. Although you may not be in control of what happens in your office, you can refrain from colluding in negative behavior. It is imperative that you find a way to act and work with others that makes you a valuable employee and ensures your own sense of integrity.

First and foremost, follow the golden rule: treat others the way you want to be treated. Of course, this approach means avoiding any rude, hurtful, or disrespectful behavior and always striving for positive, constructive interactions. Respond to e-mails promptly instead of ignoring them, and be good-natured instead of sending snarky zingers. Show your colleagues respect by praising their work sincerely and specifically. Remembering to be civil and courteous may be challenging at times, but maintaining a positive work environment will improve your bottom line—and it might just make everyone's day a bit more pleasant.

One of the most important ways to show respect for your fellow employees is to be on time to meetings and other scheduled events. Also, don't allow meetings to run over. Time is everyone's most precious commodity. If you save time for others, they will reward your display of respect.

Of course, talking about treating people correctly is easy, but keeping it up can be challenging. In careers such as documentary filmmaking, tough competition, minimal profits, and films that fail to attract an audience can create situations in which people, feeling vulnerable and scared, look out only for themselves.

In this age of instant communication, writing a disrespectful e-mail takes only two minutes, but the damage it causes can last for months or more. For example, a colleague was recently angry about how another colleague had described him. He sent a damaging, intemperate overreaction via e-mail and copied everyone: "I am suspicious of your motives because you have deliberately framed the discussion to make me look foolish, arrogant, and immature." It is always better to go see the person and discuss the matter one on one.

Civility and courtesy in the workplace aren't good just for *you*; they are good for business. Treating colleagues with honesty, sincerity, and respect creates an environment with higher morale, productivity, and efficiency. As a new college graduate just starting your career, the long-term success of your employer might not be a top priority for you, but soon the following benefits will matter to you, too:

- *Increased productivity and quality*: In business, it's easy to treat a supervisor or CEO with the utmost respect, but treating colleagues, staff, clients, and even competitors the same way is just as important to creating a productive workplace. When our hard work is praised and appreciated, we naturally want to continue to produce the highest-quality work.

- *Increased trust and teamwork*: When employees act respectfully toward one another, they learn to trust each other and begin to operate as a team. We are more inclined to work efficiently and enthusiastically if we are in an environment of positive energy, surrounded by colleagues who are considerate of our well-being. Civility and courtesy will reinforce these feelings and create a network of trust and teamwork within the company. This "we" mentality encourages us to be more thoughtful about our work, because its quality will affect our teammates and the company as a whole.

- *Increased long-term gains*: A company is only as good as its products and services, which are only as good as the employees who provide them. If a company is comprised of people who conduct themselves with respect for others, it is more likely to create high-quality products and services and in turn become a formidable force in the marketplace. A strong employee infrastructure gives businesses a competitive edge in the marketplace.

When I graduated, I had student loans to pay off—and expectations about what it meant to climb the career ladder. These factors added tremendous pressure to find and keep a job in my field. After a great deal of searching, I landed a job at a local company doing exciting work within my field of study. Although one would hope that this is where the story would end happily, it didn't.

The work environment was very negative. Employees would mock one another and treat requests for information or assistance as a sign of weakness. In addition, the most frequent subject of conversation was highly inappropriate and offensive commentary about women. Each day, during my long morning commute, I dreaded the coming workday. Despite my better judgment, and advice to the contrary, I did not quit the job. I learned to do my best to ignore the environment around me and to limit my interactions with the others. Deep breaths and reflection would ease my mind enough to start the day.

It wasn't until I was ultimately fired that I realized how much happier I would have been if I had just quit instead of worrying about my student loans or career goals. I learned that stress from a truly toxic environment isn't managed; it is lived with. Even in a bad economy, there are other opportunities, and I believe it is worth taking the risk rather than continuing to live under stress and unhappiness at work. —Will Reid, grad student

As you may have surmised by now, civility is not necessarily an end in itself. It is a means to giving yourself a more satisfying and serene professional life and to accomplishing your goals and those of your employer. In effect, what you do unto others, you do unto yourself, or, put another way, what goes around, comes around.

CHAPTER NINETEEN

~

Survive Bad Performance Reviews

Achievement seems to be connected with action. Successful men and women keep moving. They make mistakes, but they don't quit.

—Conrad Hilton

Performance reviews can either be treated as a necessary evil, something you just have to suffer through periodically at your job, or as an opportunity to touch base with reality and identify the weak spots in your work.

Maybe this year your review wasn't all that glowing, and you feel demoralized after your faults have been brought up for discussion. You don't have to respond defensively or let it eat at you. Here are some questions you can ask yourself that may help you turn a bad performance review into a positive opportunity:

- *What's the purpose of a performance review?* Remember that you're not being reviewed just to make you feel better about yourself. The purpose of the review is to make sure everyone is working at the level they should be. Sometimes this means hearing bad news. If you understand the review's purpose and try to remain as objective as you can, you'll be ready to accept bad news and turn it into positive action.
- *What's the emotion in the room?* There are two sets of emotions you should be concerned with during your performance review: yours and your manager's. Try to keep from getting defensive or angry. It won't be productive and will just make the situation worse. Instead, pay at-

72

tention to what your manager's emotions are. Is he or she delivering bad news with optimism and genuine care for your welfare? Or does the mood reflect negative, fed-up, or even rancorous feelings?

Your manager's emotions can tell you a lot about how much he or she expects of you, whether she is angling to fire you eventually, or whether he sincerely wants to nurture and mentor you so you can become a star performer.

- *What are some specific examples?* Be sure to ask your manager for specific examples of the areas in which he or she feels you can improve. Examining your own performance broadly after hearing general feedback may not be enough for you to make an effort to change. Sometimes you may know exactly what you're doing that led to the negative feedback, but not always. Make sure you understand exactly what needs to change, or you'll only be setting yourself up for another bad review.
- *What can I do next?* Thank your manager for taking the time to review your performance, then really examine his or her comments. Suggest a follow-up meeting to go over the comments if you don't understand them or how to change. Develop an action plan with your manager. Taking this initiative will show him or her that you are engaged and ready to improve.

Above all, walk out of your performance review with the purpose of setting new goals. Everyone has room for improvement, and sometimes it takes a bit of a reality check to jumpstart your effort. A bad performance review doesn't have to be such a downer. Set goals to be a better employee and to turn negative feedback into an opportunity!

Alternatively, you may be pleased with your evaluation, or even find it too glowing. Sometimes you may have to ask yourself if your manager is prone to praising too highly. In this case, try to be your toughest critic. Be pleased with your review, but ask yourself where you may have slipped up or where you could have done better. No one knows your work and abilities better than you do. Perhaps you are outperforming everyone else at your level on staff, but you know you could have done even better.

Turn reviews into opportunities. If your manager points out shortcomings in your talents or abilities, or you think you could have done an even better job despite a glowing review, ask your manager if you can take training courses or classes in particular skills or technology. Many firms budget annually for a certain amount of staff education or advanced training. A review can be a good time to raise questions about schooling that could enhance your professional worth.

If your boss turns you down for training, try to get him or her to allow you to bring up the subject again in six months. And don't take rejection personally. Some managers are opposed to allowing staff, especially during work hours, to engage in class work regardless of company policies. If your manager is one of those, you will have to come up with a good list of reasons that advanced training will benefit your company, or even your manager, specifically.

CHAPTER TWENTY

~

Become a Powerful Speaker

If you want to build a ship, don't drum up people together to collect wood and don't assign them tasks and work, but rather teach them to long for the endless immensity of the sea.

—Antoine de Saint-Exupery

At one point or another, you will have to rise into the spotlight and speak. This position can be unnerving. Let's start with some tips that hold true for almost all forms of public speaking.

General Points

One key to delivering terrific talks is to provide information about something that matters deeply to you. When you are passionate about your topic, you will feel less nervous and can avoid manipulative salesmanship and superficial techniques. Try to think of yourself as a persona when you step up to the podium. Play a role. You are no longer you but an information source, or an entertainer, or someone who will shed humor on dry data. Thinking of yourself as playing a role takes the pressure off of you as an individual. When you arrive at the podium, look out at the audience, scanning it and letting the audience look at you. If you wait a few seconds before speaking, you will capture their attention for your opening remarks.

Always focus first on *what* you are saying and *why* you are saying it—not *how*. Externals such as eye contact, hand gestures, and voice modulation are unimportant compared to identifying what lights your fire and sharing your convictions with the audience with compelling enthusiasm.

It is critical to prepare rigorously, starting with a clear notion of the key messages you want the audience to take away from your presentation. Be clear about the specific actions you would like the audience to take from your presentation.

Prepare a speech that you feel comfortable delivering. If you are unsure of what you are saying, the audience will pick up on your discomfort, which will affect how they respond to your talk. To instill confidence in yourself, go over your speech alone, speaking it out loud, using notes as necessary, and timing it to be sure it is the proper length. Practice over and over again over a course of several days so that by the time you give the speech, you will have the pace and timing down.

At the podium, it is important to connect with your audience. When you make your presentation a stimulating give-and-take, the audience feels that they are part of the presentation, and you do not feel isolated behind a lectern. This direct human connection is manifested through laughter, applause, nods, smiles of recognition, looks of concern, and questions. All of these behaviors are signs that the audience is with you.

You can reach out to the audience in many different ways, such as asking a direct question, making a startling statement, telling a story (see the next chapter), using a prop, showing a picture, eliciting laughter, distributing a handout, asking a rhetorical question, and having the audience engage in a physical activity.

Remember, when you let your inner fire ignite, you move the audience by speaking from the heart. You discover yourself to be a greater speaker than you ever dreamed yourself to be.

Having the right mind-set is half the battle. The rest has to do with preparation and ways to organize and present your material. Here are suggestions to help you excel in office presentations and in large public events.

An In-House Presentation

Within a company, staff members often need to give presentations to one another, to other departments, to senior staff, or to board members. In these cases, your audience is likely to know the basic facts or situation with which you are dealing. You may need to pull together some data about the organization or about an outside entity with which it is working, but that data should already be at hand in company computers. The accessibility of the data and your familiarity with it should speed along the process of writing your speech.

Avoid repeating information already generally known, or keep it very brief. Focus on introducing your audience to the information they do not have. Be very aware of time. Speaking engagements of this sort are usually the most tightly timed that you will encounter.

For presenting data or other information, or for using photographs or other images to illustrate points you are making, use PowerPoint or another presentation program. Such visuals will reinforce what you are saying. When using PowerPoint, each screen should have no more than twenty-five words on it. If you put up too much text, people will read it instead of listening to what you are saying. PowerPoint presentations should not be the centerpiece of your talk but an interesting and reinforcing sideshow.

Don't put text on the screen that repeats what you are saying. Use text that enlarges on what you are saying without repeating it. Repetition is another way to lose audience attention—if they recognize that the screen is merely duplicating your words, they will read it instead of listening.

Some people will take notes on the material in your PowerPoint. Try to keep an eye on people who seem to write down things when you put up a new screen. If you sense they are copying information, give them time to do so before moving to the next slide.

In all cases, keep your talk concise and sharply focused on the subject on which you were asked to speak. Allow time for questions. You may have left out information that others want, and a question-and-answer session will allow you to provide that information. Questions also will help you pinpoint shortcomings in your talk so you can polish it if you ever have to repeat it. You'll find more about question-and-answer sessions below.

Giving a Major Speech to an Unfamiliar Audience

Preparation

- Start preparing at least two months before the event. Deal with your nervousness and "butterflies" by preparing thoroughly, acting confidently, exercising, stretching, smiling, breathing deeply, practicing visualization, and having a positive mental attitude that focuses on the needs of the audience, not on yourself.
- Establish clear goals, such as advancing an agenda, producing some action, or building a stronger relationship. Write these goals with emotional juice. For example, instead of writing "Give a good speech," write "Give an electrifying speech that moves the audience to feel passionate about joining our campaign," or "Give a speech that taps deeply into my passion for conservation."

- Make one of your goals the creation of good theater that has a motivating and magical effect on your audience. Make a commitment to avoid being boring, mediocre, or colorless. Speak compellingly from your deepest convictions.

Drafting

- Begin with a brainstorming session; don't begin by drafting an outline! Instead, act like a madman and free up your inner creative-idea generator. Either electronically or on paper, quickly record all of the things you'd like to convey about your topic—be sure to capture your big ideas and passions. Only after that nonjudgmental brainstorming should you begin an outline.
- If you are not sure how to construct your speech, try finishing this sentence: "The five questions I'm most frequently asked about Topic X are . . ." Pose each question to the audience and answer it for them in a conversational manner, just as you would for someone you met at a party.
- Find interesting stories by asking yourself, *When did something go wrong? Where did I suffer?* Write it down, then cut it by 50 percent. Keep in mind that the story should not be about you, even if you are featured in it. It should be about the point you are trying to make.
- Think hard about, and focus on, the deepest concerns of your audience. Call the organizers of the event (or the presenters, if you are on a panel—see chapter 22) and find out all you can about the audience and their concerns. What's in it for them? Make sure your agenda is interwoven with the agenda of your audience.
- Appeal to something larger than the audience's self-interest. Take them to a higher level. This is your opportunity to inform them about the larger picture, to give them background on the topic, or to educate them about details of which they might not be aware. Present opposing views as fairly as possible to give yourself credibility and to generate trust.
- Don't drown your audience with excessive information. Select three main points. Decide what the real story is beneath these messages. What is the emotional journey on which you want to take the audience?
- Use observational humor. Avoid lame jokes that everybody has already heard. Instead, use observational humor as much as possible, and be self-deprecatory.
- Avoid PowerPoint slides during major speeches. PowerPoint can be a vital tool when giving talks that involve data, such as pie charts, graphs, and so on, that you are presenting to colleagues or if you are giving a speech on, for example, a historical figure or event that the

audience may want to see in photographs. However, PowerPoint slides can dilute the impact of your message if they are impersonal, tired, and mind numbing. They deflect you from your goal of painting a picture with passion and language.

Technology does not make you a great speaker. Too often, Power-Point slides are an electronic crutch to help you avoid the hard work of practice. You are giving the presentation to provide leadership and inspiration, and you are the best visual aid. PowerPoint slides distract attention from you as the focal point of the room. Before using it, ask yourself if PowerPoint slides will give your audience something you cannot otherwise provide. Use PowerPoint only if the answer is yes.

- Write out the whole speech word for word based on the outline. Never let anyone write it for you. Use simple, vivid, and conversational language, colorful metaphors, and clear, compelling evidence—thus creating a persuasive articulation of your viewpoint.
- Don't plan on reading your speech. Even a well-written speech can sound boring when read aloud. In addition, if you are looking at notes rather than at your audience, the audience will feel kept at a distance, and you will have a hard time developing a rapport with them.
- Revise your text relentlessly. Then revise it again.

Practice

- Generate a list of key points. When you have created a solid version of your speech, generate a list of key points in brief sentences—sometimes called bits or talking points. These bits are all you will have with you on stage.
- Practice your presentation out loud as much as possible, as mentioned earlier. Ask a colleague to give you feedback and criticism. Rehearse, rehearse, rehearse.

Delivery

- Warm up. Before going on stage, warm up your mouth and face by saying out loud over and over again, in private, "enough of this animalistic anthropomorphizing theatricality." Or say the vowels of the alphabet over and over again.
- Meet and greet audience members before your presentation. Not only will this encourage the audience to feel a closer connection with you, but it also will make you less nervous and self-conscious when you begin your talk.
- Grab the audience's attention. Start your presentation with something that will engage the audience powerfully, such as a compelling

and relevant self-deprecatory anecdote. You have something of great value to say, and the audience is waiting to feel your intensity and personal voltage.

- While speaking, make eye contact with one person at a time for three to five seconds. Don't scan the audience. In a sense you are talking one on one and establishing a relationship with individual members of the audience. Your goal is to establish a sustained human connection with your listeners.
- Be energetic, enthusiastic, and passionate. Convey a high level of commitment and sincerity. Show you care and that you have convictions. Project vocal energy. Make a total commitment to the immediacy of the moment. Be physical. Gesticulate.
- Move closer to the audience. Traditional podium speaking is no longer adequate. Walk into the audience if possible.
- Use props as much as possible. Hold up things—newspapers, articles, flyers, money, anything.
- Use the power of pauses. Don't be afraid of silence. Eloquent pauses build interest and suspense.
- Encourage audience participation. Let them tell you their stories. Get the audience to offer solutions. Encourage questions.
- Encourage next steps. Ask the audience to write down the first step they will take before they leave the room. Your presentation will be successful if you motivate your audience to do something. It isn't what you say that matters but what the audience hears, feels, and does.
- Take audience questions *before* the end of your presentation. Ending on Q&As yields a weak wrap-up. After Q&As, end with a stirring call to action or a favorite story that makes a compelling point.
- Actively listen to what the audience members are asking. Check your understanding by restating questions from the audience. Restating confirms that you really understand their question and ensures that they and the rest of the audience feel heard and involved in the presentation. Use their names if you know them.
- Don't go overtime. Ever.
- Prepare a handout that recaps your speech so the learning is reinforced.

Learning to give good speeches is like learning to ride a bicycle. At first you may feel a bit shaky, but with practice you will become a steady and smooth speaker, and speaking will become fun. Even a consummate public speaker such as John F. Kennedy had to undergo training and experience before he became the moving orator he was.

~

CHAPTER TWENTY-ONE

Use Stories Effectively

All great literature is one of two stories; a man goes on a journey or a stranger comes to town.

—Leo Tolstoy

One thing you might want to try in your speeches—as well as in more routine presentations—is storytelling.

A great story changes our understanding of the world. It gives us new and deeper insights into our own lives and the lives of other people. Stories help us make sense of everything we see around us. They also contain the power to captivate audiences.

The hero's journey, or the narrative of the hero archetype, is the fundamental story of human struggle and triumph. In Western culture, the hero story is modeled after the myth of Theseus, who sought out and killed the Minotaur in the labyrinth of Crete. The significance of this point is that hero stories often are about brave souls who undertake very difficult and dangerous tasks. In other words, the stakes are high.

The hero wins over the audience because he or she maintains the high moral ground, which connects humankind to what is decent and good. But heroes are not perfect, which enables us to relate to them as human beings. A hero is courageous despite fear and failings. The audience also is inclined to root for the hero because we like to cheer for the underdog who is going through a difficult endeavor.

To tell a compelling hero story in your speech, make sure to include the three phases of the hero's journey:

1. The hero seizes an opportunity and takes the journey, breaking away from ingrained habits, routines, and habitual ways of thinking and taking a risk. It takes courage to take this leap. The hero crosses a threshold and begins a search for new ways of being, thinking, and perceiving.

2. The hero faces the challenge, ready to confront frightening obstacles and barriers, to battle internal and external enemies, and often losing but never giving up. The hero perseveres until victory is found. Mentors and coaches weigh in, new opportunities are created, and the hero's abilities are stretched to the breaking point.

   Defeats and setbacks happen over and over again. There might well be some supreme ordeal—physical, emotional, spiritual, or psychological—in which the hero's life is threatened and hangs in the balance. Such an ordeal might be an inner quest for truth, wisdom, and fulfillment. Although the hero is suffering and exhausted, he or she also is growing emotionally in new and dramatic ways. A transformation is taking place.

3. The hero finds the victory, integrating what he or she has learned into a new life and a new way of being and, in doing so, transforming his or her life into something inspiring. Victory does not always mean succeeding in the conventional sense. It may mean finding some internal victory—perhaps overcoming flaws and self-doubts and living by better, more altruistic values.

   In this phase, the hero creates a new life embodying increased wisdom and transforms in some way, often on the inside. Self-discovery has occurred. The hero is a different person from when he or she started and has achieved self-understanding and inner tranquility.

The hero's journey has a beginning, middle, and end. It has compelling characters, rising tension, and conflicts that reach a resolution of some kind. It engages the audience on an intellectual and emotional level, inspiring listeners to want to know what happens next, to change their own lives, and to demand changes in society. This is the essence of a great story. An excellent book on how to tell effective stories is *Connections* by Randy Olson, Dorie Barton, and Brian Palermo.

~

CHAPTER TWENTY-TWO

Moderate Panels Effectively

By failing to prepare, you are preparing to fail.

—Benjamin Franklin

You might be called upon to moderate a panel, which is a great opportunity to shine and to practice your leadership and speaking skills. Generally, panels focus on a single topic. Each member of the panel gives a few brief remarks on the subject, then the panel is open to questions from the audience. The questioner usually picks the panel member from whom he or she wants an answer, but choosing may be left to the moderator.

As a moderator, your responsibility is to ensure that the panel works as a unit and that individual presentations complement one another and avoid overlap. Your goal is to exercise leadership so that the audience walks away saying, "The panel was fantastic," not "Was that me or you I heard snoring?"

Here are ten steps to take to make sure you have a presentation that is informative and interesting to the audience and satisfying to the panelists:

1. Preparation is the key to a great panel presentation. At least a month prior to the panel, tell members when and where to turn up, how to shape their comments, and how long they have to speak.
2. Three weeks before the event, provide questions to the panelists, then hold a conference call to discuss questions, individual approaches, and ground rules.

3. Get the panelists together for a short meeting before the event so that everyone feels comfortable with one another and understands each other's viewpoint. When possible, conduct this meeting in person. A conference call also works.

4. Work hard on the introduction of each speaker. If you can tell a humorous story about each one, so much the better.

5. Your prime job as moderator is control. You have to control content, flow, time, and questions. Never allow any panelist to dominate, exceed time limits, or stray from the topic. You are abdicating your responsibilities as moderator and harming the other panelists if you allow anyone to go into overtime.

6. Do not allow an audience member to steal the spotlight. Apportion audience questions among the panelists. Start and end on time. Be authoritative—interrupt panelists if you have to.

7. To avoid the potential embarrassment of a silent audience, prepare a few questions to kick-start the discussion.

8. If two or more people raise their hands at the same time, reassure the people not selected that you won't forget to come back to them for their questions later. Protect the soft-spoken and inarticulate.

9. Reserve 30 to 50 percent of the time for audience participation, and ask every questioner to give his or her name and affiliation. Repeat each question in your own words to the whole audience.

10. End the session by giving a coherent summary of what has been said and by thanking the panelists and the audience. Afterward, send each panelist a thank-you note.

Panel presentations sink or swim on your leadership as the moderator, on your interpersonal skills, and on your ability to provoke a stimulating discussion. If you do your homework, prepare your panelists, and stay on top of the panelists' remarks and the audience's questions, you will have a successful panel presentation.

PART V

~

MAKE MEANINGFUL CONNECTIONS

A good networker has two ears and one mouth and uses them proportionately.

—Ivan Misner

The richest people in the world look for and build networks, everyone else looks for work.

—Robert Kiyosaki

What should my "elevator speech" include? How do I convey my excitement for my projects and get others on board? Networking terrifies me, so I avoid it—how can I find it more enjoyable? How do I raise money for my projects?

CHAPTER TWENTY-THREE

~

Have Your Elevator Speech Ready

I will prepare and some day my chance will come.

—Abraham Lincoln

Imagine this: You're next in a long queue of businessmen and women waiting to pitch their brilliant ideas to a top executive and secure future collaboration opportunities. You have forty-five seconds to give a brief summary or make a brief request—an elevator speech.

What do you say?

How do you say it?

And how do you prevent yourself from being just another face in the crowd?

This is what the elevator speech is all about.

Elevator speeches, if used effectively, take advantage of short bursts of opportunity. They are the auditions of the business world. You need to come up with a way to maximize your impact in front of your audience and make a lasting impression that will get you another meeting. The chance to give an elevator speech can happen at any time, anywhere. If you're feeling unprepared, don't fear. Here are ten simple tips to help you prepare your own elevator speech:

1. *Start with the basics.* This may seem a no-brainer, but make sure that you're aware of and can execute public speaking skills confidently and fluently. Make eye contact, breathe regularly, speak confidently, and pace the flow

of your words. Try to answer in two or three sentences these questions about your subject: who, what, when, where, why, and how.

2. *Use positive, strong language.* Wishy-washy language gets you nowhere when you are conducting a business transaction. Use confident language such as "will" and "can" instead of "might" or "could."

3. *Practice.* To feel the most comfortable delivering your speech, you need to practice. Repetition will get you to the point where you can pitch at a moment's notice.

4. *Don't be mechanical.* Although you want to be prepared, you don't want to appear stiff or rehearsed. In her *Forbes* article "The Perfect Elevator Pitch to Land a Job," contributor Nancy Collamer suggests you be flexible and responsive to your particular audience. Tailor your words to match what you know of the person to whom you are speaking.

5. *Let your personality shine.* You are not just another talking head. What makes your business voice unique?

6. *Talk with your audience, not at them.* Conversations are a two-way street. Make sure you leave some space for your audience to respond to you and to encourage engagement with and attention to your pitch.

7. *Go easy on details.* Because you have limited time, it's necessary to get to the meat of your idea quickly. In the *Nature* article "Communication: Two Minutes to Impress," writer Roberta Kwok suggests that people "consider the big picture" and leave out inessential details.

8. *Use universal language.* Don't leave your audience out in the cold by using technical language. *Forbes* contributor Nancy Collamer notes that technical language puts you at risk of making your audience "feel stupid or uninformed"—not to mention distracted.

9. *Be appreciative.* An elevator speech is essentially a request for resources and time. Make sure that you demonstrate your appreciation of your audience's consideration before and after your pitch by thanking them.

10. *Leave a calling card.* Your speech can be impressive and intriguing, but all your efforts will be for naught if you don't make plans to follow up. Exchange contact information via a business card, if possible, and state your intentions for reestablishing contact.

Elevator speeches are essential across industries, from media to finance and beyond.

Opportunities are gained and lost by elevator speeches. By being prepared and relaxed, you can increase greatly your chance of acquiring more business opportunities at networking events and during serendipitous meetings. These tips will send you on your way.

~

CHAPTER TWENTY-FOUR

Build Relationships through Networking

What keeps so many people back is simply the unwillingness to pay the price, to make the exertion, the effort to sacrifice their ease and comfort.

—Orison Swett Marden

Networking is an essential skill for professionals who want to grow their careers. Making new business friends can lead to fresh ideas, useful information, new partnerships, and increased income. Networking is about being authentic, unselfish, genuine, and honest. It is about building relationships and trust. Although social media such as LinkedIn can help you make initial connections, it is face-to-face communication that truly builds relationships.

Develop a reputation as an unselfish, decent person with whom other people would want to work. Become a resource for others. Look for ways you can help other people make useful contacts. Put in a good word for others. Treat everyone with respect and courtesy, especially those less powerful than you.

One way to network is to contact people who can help you meet your goals. Identify successful people, both VIPs and the not-so-famous, whom you want to meet for advice, ideas, inspiration, information, money, and deals. Go out of your way to meet them. Ask them specific questions. Find ways to offer help and assistance.

Events and receptions are another terrific place to network. They give you an opportunity to meet many people who have similar interests and who can be helpful and supportive to you and your work. You may not often get an opportunity to connect with these people, so make sure you get the most out of these events with the following tips:

- *Before attending a networking opportunity, think strategically about your goals.* Produce and write down five goals you have for this event, beginning with such questions as What are your expected outcomes? What results do you want? Do you want to find work? Learn about a specific company? Find a specific kind of job? Find a summer internship? Extend your network of contacts? Gain insight into your career choices? Find career inspiration? Meet people in the industry and get their business cards? Give out your résumé? Sell an idea? Get advice and help? Meet a key person? Arrange a follow-up meeting with that key person? What else? Be as specific as possible.
- *Go out of your way to meet people.* Physically move around and work the room. Don't get stuck talking to one person just to be polite. When it's time to move on to meet another, say to the person, "I enjoyed meeting you and learning about your work. Let's both meet some of the other people here. I hope to run into you again later." Then shake hands and move on.
- *Reach out to people in a warm and sincere way.* Show genuine interest in everyone you meet. Go out of your way to introduce new friends to old friends.
- *Be curious and listen well.* When you meet someone, smile, shake hands firmly, make eye contact, and ask open-ended questions. Resist the urge to dominate the conversation. Focus on the other person's interests and concerns, not yours. Listen intently. Be present. Learn the person's name and use it so you begin to associate the name with the face.

As an introvert, I've always had difficulty networking. Eventually I realized that 90 percent of networking isn't about being extroverted—it's about being a pleasant person. The more honest I was as a conversationalist, the better impression I left and the more references I got for jobs. —Alexander Gillies, grad student

- *Act with confidence even if you feel shy and intimidated.* You may feel understandably self-conscious and uncomfortable when meeting people more powerful and successful than you are, but successful networking requires you to do it anyway. Do your best to appear self-confident and try to ignore any negative self-talk. Don't waste time and energy fretting over someone else who may be more successful at networking than you are. We all go through ups and downs. Just concentrate on being the best you can be.

- *When you talk about your work, talk passionately.* Prepare a one-minute description of what you do or want to do so that you are ready to talk in a succinct, enthusiastic, and inspiring way about your work and ideas (see the previous chapter on elevator speeches).
- *Take good notes.* During the event, be a sponge and soak up as much learning as you can, taking good mental notes. Immediately following the event, write down all the information and ideas you've gleaned so that you can act on them.
- *Develop an action plan to follow up after the event.* When you get home, write down the action items and ideas that you are going to work on to improve yourself and further develop your career. What websites, books, articles, organizations, and people are you going to follow up with?
- *After meeting an interesting person, send a thank-you note.* Suggest ways you might be able to help that individual and his or her business. Fulfill any promises you made. Show people that you do what you say you're going to do. In your thank-you notes, can you suggest ways you might be able to help your new contacts? What offers can you make to raise new possibilities for people? Don't let the risk of rejection stop you from creating new ideas and offering them.
- *Don't forget to have fun!* Smile, be happy (or at least act happy), and spread joy and goodwill.

Once you become comfortable with networking—which you will with practice and repetition—you will find that it is one of the more pleasant aspects of career building. Networking is much the same as making new friends, and some professional contacts will become friends. Keep in mind that you are not out to exploit the people with whom you network. You want to offer them something—your talents, skills, and dreams.

When I was going to meet a person who had my dream job, someone told me, "Go in thinking you want to like him or her, and that person will like you back." It is the simplest but best advice I have ever had. I prepare a lot beforehand, of course, but I can know only so much about a person and a company. Thinking that I am going to meet someone interesting and enjoy myself relieves the tension and makes the person become simply another human being.

I now do this every time I have to meet someone I find slightly intimidating. Before each meeting I research as much as I can about the person and his company, and I write down a few questions for him. Then I think about what would be the simplest element that would make the meeting successful. That is usually something like, "He says he loves my idea and is interested in helping me," or "She puts me in touch with more people," or even "I now understand something about the business that helps me in my career decisions."

Once I have my goals down, I remember that I am going to have a good time. The more people I meet, the more relaxed I am, and the better the meetings go. It took me a while to realize that it is actually a lot of fun to meet with people who have similar interests and different experiences.
—grad student

~

CHAPTER TWENTY-FIVE

Raise Money Successfully

Nothing great was ever achieved without enthusiasm.

—Ralph Waldo Emerson

One way to advance your career is to know how to raise money. At some point, perhaps soon, you will need to get funding for one of your projects. The ability to raise funds successfully is something that can easily set you apart from other candidates applying for the same job.

Fund-raising can be one of the most daunting and intimidating parts of any project. In the case of many professionals, the role of fund-raiser can feel way out of sync with who you are and the work you do. Artists such as filmmakers tend to be passionate, creative people who want to express their stories or shed light on important issues, but they often have no experience in sales and no desire to become slick salesmen.

The good news is that the same creativity and passion that will make you successful in an artistic career also will make you adept at fund-raising. Here are four steps you can take:

1. *Identify potential donors.* The first step in fund-raising is finding and identifying potential donors. In some ways, this step can seem the most difficult. However, if you start with friends, family, and business contacts and then continue to be always on the lookout for potential donors, you will find them. Be alert at all times; constantly seek out

potential donors. Ask your existing donors to introduce you to friends who might want to donate to your cause or project.

This process may feel uncomfortable at first. It is important to remember that you are not tricking anyone, and you are not selling him or her something unneeded. You are also not approaching them as someone in need of charity. Your project is, in one way or another, solving a problem, changing lives, and transforming society for the better, and you are offering them the chance to be involved in a noble cause. If you are dealing with a foundation or other funding entity, remind yourself that the staffs of these places are in the business of donating funds to causes and that you are guiding them toward and informing them about a cause that may capture their interest—*you* are helping *them*.

2. *Present your project in a compelling way.* It is absolutely essential that you not only believe in your project, but that you are able to express what makes it compelling. You are inspiring funders to join you in being part of an important project.

   Think about how to present your project as an exciting challenge or vision. Ask yourself: How will your project make a difference in the world? Why are you uniquely qualified to undertake this effort? If you think about fund-raising in these terms, you will not only feel more comfortable with the process of appealing for money, but you will also be more successful at it.

My friends and I once put together a Kickstarter campaign for a series of music videos that interconnected to tell a continuous story. It was an intriguing concept, but our campaign suffered from one big problem: We didn't tell anyone the story. Donors didn't just want to hear about an idea; they wanted an idea with a good story behind it—something that drew them in, something to which they could relate. We didn't meet our goal, but it served as a great learning experience. —Alexander Gillies, grad student

3. *Develop a good relationship with the donor.* Just as important as the value and importance of your project is your ability to connect with the donor. You must develop a relationship and earn not only your donors' interest but also their trust and respect. Listen to them, learn about what is most important to them, and let them get to know you.

Having a strong relationship will make it much easier when it comes time to ask for money. You will already know the person's interests, his or her priorities, and the appropriate amount to ask for.

Always ask for a specific amount (rather than a range) for a specific project. The most important part of asking is simply having the courage to ask, but you also must be patient and listen to the donor. Even if the donor cannot make a gift at the time you make your request, remain positive and understanding. Keep the door open for the future.

4. *Keep the donor informed about your project.* Once a donor does agree to support your project, your job is just beginning. It is critical that you stay in close contact. Call immediately to tell her that you appreciate her generosity, then write a warm, thoughtful thank-you note. As time goes on, keep in contact by sending updates, scripts, articles, or whatever you have to keep her involved.

Create a system to remind yourself to make regular contact. It is important that no donor feels used or that you only built a relationship in order to get money.

After receiving a gift, make a point of seeing the donor again soon and do not ask for anything more.

When you can build a compelling case for the importance of your project and develop real relationships with donors, you will be successful at fundraising. If you do it right, everyone will feel like they've won, because they are part of something great that is going to make a difference in the world.

Afterword

By reading this book and absorbing its lessons, you have taken a major step toward your successful transition to the post-college world.

Remember Paige Jones, Kevin Borow, Jacob Motz, and Berna Elibuyuk from the preface? They are advancing in their careers, but doing so hasn't been easy for any of them.

Paige writes:
I'm doing well—staying plenty busy, that's for sure. I've been working at *The Frederick News-Post* in Frederick County, Maryland, for six months now (since June 2014) as the nighttime crime reporter.

After applying to about fifty job openings starting at the end of March right up to graduation, I did a handful of interviews and was offered this position the day before my commencement ceremony. My parents were absolutely ecstatic and relieved, but I wasn't entirely sure I wanted to work as a crime reporter, especially while I was interviewing for a position that seemed to be more in the realm of my dream career.

I was dubious about my job after starting in June—I was the "baby of the newsroom" at twenty-one, whereas most of my colleagues were in their late twenties and newlyweds. Plus, working at night from 2:30 to 11:30 p.m., while all my friends and my boyfriend worked normal hours, made it hard to socialize and even harder to stay awake as a morning person!

Six months later, I enjoy my job, but it's not something I'd like to do long term. I see myself moving on eventually, but I enjoy what I do now, have the energy to do it, and learn so many new things every day. In the past week, I've covered two homicides, interviewed a woman now recovering from bile-duct cancer after doctors told her they could do no more, and wrote a story about a man who rides along with city police every Christmas Eve. I typically talk to people in the worst moments of their lives (car crashes, fires, etc.) and write that up for the next day's paper, which can be physically and emotionally draining. But I feel blessed that these people invite me into their lives and trust me to tell their story, and that is what motivates me to go into work every day, not knowing what that day could bring.

Kevin Borow writes:

I'm doing well! After graduation in May 2014, I stayed in Washington, D.C., working at a restaurant to save as much money as I could. I relocated to Los Angeles in early October and started working at an internship in November with AEF&H Talent, a small, boutique talent agency that represents some pretty well-known actors. I found that it's very difficult to find a job in LA without experience. A classroom can teach only so much, so a few months at an internship is a wonderful way, if not the only way, to get started!

One of the assistants left the agency in January 2015, and the firm hired me as her replacement. I'm busier than I've ever been, but I'm learning more every day. Being an assistant is a rough job with long hours and low earnings, but that is how you pay your dues to move up.

At the agency, you get to see the inner workings of the industry and learn much more than you could while sitting in a classroom. After a year or two, most assistants are ready to move up in the agency world or go on to a different aspect of the industry. All it takes is time and experience. We'll see how long it takes me to move up. I've found that if you put in the work and give something everything you've got, people will notice. I'm still figuring out where I want to be, but it's all a process, and I believe I'm heading down the right road.

Jacob Motz writes:

After a few months of working on personal projects and fruitless applications, I happily landed a position at a media company in downtown Washington, D.C. I spend my days shooting and editing and often travel to far-off locations such as Miami to create short-form digital content for construction magazines. It is a fresh college grad's dream job! But I couldn't have done it without my friend at the company tipping me off to the opening, which proves that, in college and in life, sometimes it doesn't matter what you know but who you know.

Berna Elibuyuk writes:

After my difficulties in getting a job or even an internship, I pulled myself together and decided to build an online portfolio. I established myself as a freelance visual designer and videographer. Many people from around the world liked my work and commissioned multiple projects.

A year and a half after graduating, I returned to school for a master's degree in film and electronic media. Now, as I sit in my graduate classes, I have to reassure myself that something good will come from all this hard work and determination. But I know it's really up to me to stand and be heard. I can't just sit and wait for positions to come to me. I have to enter the real world and talk to people, learn more about what they do, and see if I can interest them in my work. It's a matter of communicating and building a broad social circle that will be strong enough to help me in my career search.

We're all so immersed in the tech age that we tend to forget about the spoken word. But our text will all look the same to people working behind computers at human-resources departments. It's up to us to make contact with people. We have to take action and show them that we are just as capable of doing great work as the next guy who walks in for an interview.

In the face of rejection, don't lose your determination. In the wake of discouragement, continue to create exceptional work. Even if you can't score a position that relates to your degree major, you will keep yourself confident and motivated. Think of that current job as more experience to add to your résumé and as a chance to create good connections. The road to success includes many diversions.

In ending this book, I offer you three essential points:

1. First, dream big and hold fast to your dreams.
2. Second, set audacious goals.
3. Third, devote your life to a worthy cause.

Oliver Wendell Holmes put it well: "Alas for those who never sing, But die with all their music in them."

~

Examples of Personal Mission Statements

Personal Mission Statement by a Master of Fine Arts Student

Roles: A person who recognizes the power of self-improvement, son, brother, boyfriend, friend, environmentalist, filmmaker, mountain biker, world citizen

As a person who recognizes the importance of self-improvement, I will work toward achieving a high level of productivity, with both productive and leisure time working for me toward personal, social, and professional fulfillment.

Personal: I will keep promises. I will wake up on time. I will read for pleasure and personal enrichment. I will limit the amount of time I spend on unproductive activities such as watching TV shows unrelated to my career path or watching online bike videos to excess. I will avoid YouTube black holes. However, I will maintain a healthy balance between work and occasional leisure time, and I will ensure that this leisure time enriches me.

I will work out at least twice every week and maintain a high level of physical fitness, not least because I have struggled with depression in the past, and staying fit and active releases happy hormones. Although I do not currently have trouble with depression, it's important to recognize my hereditary propensity for it and to continue to be smart about active strategies to decrease any likelihood of recurrence. Recurrence of depression could have a hugely detrimental impact on my personal and professional goals.

Professional: I will keep promises. I will continue to consume lots of content related to the field I hope to enter (wildlife and environmental filmmaking); however, I will look at this content with a more critical eye toward how impressive work was created technically and how some work may have stretched or broken the rigorous filmmaking ethics I have set for myself. I will be sure to maintain these high ethical standards as I create and collaborate on films.

I will ask myself seriously whether and how every professional endeavor I undertake furthers my goal to become a wildlife filmmaker. If an opportunity does not further these goals, I will learn how to say no without damaging relationships.

I will learn new skills, including Adobe Premiere and After Effects; effective lighting techniques with a wide array of locations and lighting equipment; seamless camera movement; and effective telephoto videography. I also will familiarize myself with as many different cameras and other equipment (audio!) as possible. Film school is exactly my opportunity to learn all of these things, and I will take advantage of that.

As a son, I will talk to my parents every week on the phone. I will talk to them more than once a week at least every other week. I will e-mail them at least two to three times per week, even if just a small note to ask how their day was. I will make a point to return home to visit at least three times a year, even if I move farther away than Washington, D.C., in the future. I will be sure to stay up-to-date on their activities, hopes, and dreams, instead of blabbing on about my own so much. I will plan a trip for just my mom and me. I will go mountain biking with my dad.

As a brother, I will see my sister at least once every week. I will make a stronger effort to see her and her husband on the weekends and to spend quality time with them doing things we all enjoy. I also will accompany them to things such as theater performances or ballet, which may not usually be something I attend but they enjoy and would like to share with me.

As a boyfriend, I will support my girlfriend throughout her year and a half abroad. This will involve texting her every day—I will text her when I wake up and before I go to sleep. I will Skype with her four times a week or more. I will e-mail her three times a week or more. I will remind her just how much I love her, without bringing up too often how much I miss her. I will go above and beyond her expectations when she returns from her travels. I will organize an awesome welcome-home party. I will listen attentively and actively to her needs. I will respect her views even when they don't agree with mine, and I will work actively to see where she is coming from. I will engage with her professional work in a more comprehensive manner and help her build a strong personal and professional network, because I know she has already done this for me and will continue to do it. I will go to Uganda to visit her when she is there.

As a friend, I will keep promises. I will maintain and create new meaningful friendships that are based on mutual interests and respect. I will not fill my time with displacement activities, with friends or alone. I will get outside with my friends and encourage them to try new activities (mountain biking!) without being too pushy. I will stay in better contact with distant friends. I will not let text or e-mail conversations drop. I will avoid duplicity in my dealings with friends. If I can't make it somewhere, or simply don't feel like it, I will be honest about the reasons why.

As an environmentalist, I will not eat meat. I will discuss my enjoyment of vegetarianism with meat eaters and encourage them to consider eating less meat. I will engage in local environmental issues such as water quality and will volunteer my time for something like a river cleanup. I will keep an open and creative mind about outreach projects and actions I can take relating to the conservation issues I explore in future films. I will stay informed about environmental issues and actively discuss how those issues affect my personal circles and me. I will consider the impacts of my consumption of goods. I will continue to support local agriculture through farm shares and farmers' markets. I will cook more and eat out less. I will ride my bike more instead of taking Ubers.

As a filmmaker, I will relentlessly pursue projects that inform and inspire about the importance of protecting or restoring the natural world. I will use film as a force for good. I will hone my skills in film school and tirelessly improve them. I will create a meaningful network of contacts in the industry. I will successfully crowdfund a film project in the next year. I will reach out to my personal circles and those of my contacts to establish a potential funding base for these projects.

As a mountain biker, I will ride every week. I will ride my bike more around the city to improve riding fitness and decrease my carbon footprint. I will ride on a stationary bike every week that I don't get in a good fitness ride. I will volunteer for Trips for Kids. I will finish building my new downhill bike and ride it at least twice a month over the summer. I will discover four new riding spots this season. I will encourage friends to ride with me and reconnect with old riding buddies. I will go riding with my dad.

As a world citizen, I will stay informed on the news every day. I will continue to learn about and seek out new films, shows, podcasts, music, and performances. I will drop the ones that don't do anything for me. I will acknowledge homeless people when they ask me for money, even if it's to say that I can't help them right now. I will travel to a country outside the United States every year and much more than that if possible. I will not let commuters or tourists annoy me. They have just as much right to be here as I do. I will speak up when friends or acquaintances use derogatory humor. I will be genuine but courteous in my dealings with other people.

Personal Mission Statement by a College Junior

I want to be remembered as someone who brings joy to a room, someone who has an infectious laugh, someone who lives for adventure, someone with strong morals and values, someone who cherishes family and friends, someone who will always lend a hand, and someone who lives simply, happily, and with pure goodness.

I will always strive for personal, physical, and mental improvement. I will be devoted to my roles in my family, and with my friends and community. I will always be someone who helps, listens, and comforts others.

I will not harp on the negatives. All experiences have a purpose and meaning. I will learn from these experiences and continue on with strength and confidence. I will not give excuses. I will own up to my shortcomings and do my best to improve them. I will be more active, write diligently in my journal, meditate, and seek counseling to help improve my mental state.

I will set ambitious goals. I will not get overwhelmed, anxious, or frustrated. I will find challenge and peacefulness from attempting or accomplishing these goals.

I will be an active force in my community. I will be the change I wish to see. I will not be a hypocrite; I will take action and hold true to my morals and values.

Steps to overcome challenges:

- Be less anxious—don't overstress.
- Stop focusing on negatives.
- Accept being uncomfortable.
- Live a healthy lifestyle—eat healthy, exercise, and spend time outdoors.
- Read for myself.
- Be more loving.
- Smile always—always laugh and be more confident.
- Set aside time for creativity.
- Speak up more.

Most important things:

- My friends and family.
- My health and well-being.
- Balancing work and personal life.
- Enjoying life—finding what makes me happiest.
- Accomplishing a positive change in the world.
- Caring and showing affection to loved ones.
- Being my best self—successfully, morally, and educationally.
- Being a positive role model for others.
- Being more active in the community—volunteering and helping others in need.

Self-development and Renewal: I need to take care of myself before I exert an effort to help and take care of others. I want to be my best self: physically, emotionally, and mentally. I want to live a happy and fulfilled life. These are the steps I need to take.

Physical: I will have a plant-based diet with as much locally sourced and organic food as possible. I will make sure to set aside time for exercise. I'll go on a long run every weekend and take an exercise class once a month. I'll focus on improving my strength, flexibility, balance, posture, and endurance to ensure an energetic and active lifestyle.

Social and emotional: I will reconnect with old friends. I will be a source of positivity, laughter, inspiration, and fun. I will make an effort to connect more deeply with friends and family. I will share my feelings and thoughts more often and make sure to take control of my problems (not blame anyone else). I will be a great listener, will offer thoughtful advice, and always will be sincere.

Mental: I will read more books and articles outside of school. I will continue my education through personal projects. I will find positive role models for inspiration and encouragement. I will seek out mentors who care about me and have thoughtful advice.

Spiritual: I will define a meaning and purpose in my life. I will be hard working, courageous, patient, adventurous, creative, responsible, passionate, confident, and fearless. I will be my best self and strive to leave lasting impressions of positivity, confidence, and hope for others.

Most important roles:

- My role as a sister.
- My role as a girlfriend and friend.
- My role as a daughter and granddaughter.
- My role as a role model and leader.
- My role as an environmental activist.

Personal Mission Statement by a College Senior

I will be a productive, happy, and successful person. I will continue to create and develop long-standing and meaningful relationships with the people I interact with. I will have a successful and impactful career doing something that I love. I strive to find peace with myself and those around me.

I will seek to better the world by aiding those in need to the best of my ability and by protecting those who cannot protect themselves. I will be kind and compassionate to everyone I meet and will be helpful and courteous to them.

I will continue to improve my relationship with my sister and try to be present and supportive to my family during times of struggle and celebration. I will continue to participate in my hobbies and find ways to make them a part of my weekly routine.

I will take care of my body and my mind. I know both are fragile and need more care than average. I will be mindful of my limits and reach out to others when I am in need of aid. I will face my fears and refuse to give up just because something is distasteful or nerve-racking.

I will continue to learn about everything I can. I will allow my curiosity to flourish and will express my creativity in any way that feels right. I will find things and people that make me happy and seek them out on a regular basis.

I will set and reach goals. I will look for solutions rather than focusing on problems. I will seek resolution and compromise. I will stand up for myself. I will not be ashamed of showing fear or sadness.

I will look to improve constantly in all walks of life. I will encourage myself, and I will point out my strengths to myself rather than recognizing only my weaknesses. I will push myself, and I will learn not always to be negative. I will work on looking at the world with less cynicism. I will learn to love my family, my life, and myself.

Personal Mission Statement by a College Senior

I want to be a person who is known to be responsible, kind, funny, adventurous, curious, and willing to follow my passions fearlessly. I want to know that my work has helped contribute to the making of a more just, safe, and livable world and that my work also has helped or inspired others to do the same.

I will live my life one day at a time while also consciously thinking, but not worrying, about what comes next. I want to see the world and absorb it. I want to capture the beauty of the natural world through photography and help to protect and cherish it.

Photography is an important part of my life, and it always will be. I will use my photography to help advocate for environmental and social issues. As has been said before, my camera is a tool that helps me learn how to see without my camera.

Travel is my inspiration. I will live in different cities and places around the country and around the world. I will not be a tourist but rather a traveler—one who seeks to learn from new cultures and new places.

I will value my family and friends more than status or money. My time with family is irreplaceable, and I will take advantage of any opportunity to spend time with my mom, dad, brother, or sister.

I will treat others with kindness and respect. I will seek collaboration and partnership with those whose work I value and admire. I will pursue my own creative projects because I am passionate about them and because I want to make a difference. Time is my most precious commodity, and I will live with the vigor and passion that taking advantage of it requires. I will choose to live life as an adventure.

Personal Mission Statement by an Environmental Studies Master's Student

I will strive to improve and better myself as a person. I wish to be thought of as a moral, genuine, welcoming person who is educated with a strong, reliable work ethic and a great sense of humor. I want to be remembered as having produced a positive, enjoyable influence on the relationships I have with family, friends, and colleagues. I will live a full life, devoted to my family in my role as a daughter, sister, cousin, and granddaughter. I will support my friends in their own life accomplishments by helping them find their own version of happiness. I will provide professional guidance to my colleagues and students, sharing personal advice that I have found beneficial to myself as well as encouraging them to act toward fulfilling their own goals.

I will practice saying no to projects that I cannot fully complete to the best of my ability and to situations that will not use my time productively. I will not be afraid or guilty when saying no. I also will refuse unnecessary things that I will not need or use.

I will practice my public speaking skills by talking to large crowds and classes. I will introduce myself and meet new people.

I will be more articulate and practice patience in order to voice accurately what I want to say. I will be more clear and transparent when discussing my true passions and feelings. I will actively listen whenever anyone is speaking to me. I will remain patient and open-minded when debating.

I will travel more. I will visit Scotland as well as Denmark and other Scandinavian nations. I will learn more about other perspectives and cultures.

I will continually act to improve upon the goals I have set, and I will progress toward keeping all of my commitments and values presented in this personal mission statement.

Physical: I will exercise to improve my health and keep an overall positive feeling of well-being. I will practice my skills as a yogi, regular runner, and athlete. I will follow soccer leagues locally and internationally. I will adjust my schedule to include important necessary amounts of sleep in a comfortable, peaceful environment.

I will eat more vegetables! I will eat more produce! I will eat less meat, and eat less overall. I will try my best to consume healthy foods and to avoid toxic, low-nutrient foods. I will purchase foods and products that support ethical and moral causes with which I agree. I will set a regular time for cooking and learning new recipes and techniques. I will feed and give to others.

Social/Emotional: I will enjoy my time spent with my parents. I will listen to their stories of how they raised our family. I will have my own family and be a mother myself. I will have a dog. I will share my love with all of my family. I will bring happiness and joy to my brothers and cousins. I will continue to welcome my brother's new wife into our family. I will not fight with my other brother. I will be patient with family disputes. I will encourage family and friends always to better themselves and their relationships, and I will remind them that complaining is not a solution.

I will call my grandmother every two weeks. I will call or e-mail my other grandparents every two weeks. I will be grateful to all of my grandparents for starting families I am proud to be from. I will honor the work they have done.

I will be available and supportive to my three closest friends from college. I will be the best aunty I can be to my friend's expected baby. I will be sure to talk to each of these friends on the phone once a month.

I will support my boyfriend to accomplish his goals. I will be considerate and loving in the day-to-day routine we share. I will be patient and open-minded when we disagree. I will be an extraordinary best friend and partner to him.

Mental: I will apply myself to all potential, promising opportunities to better myself and to reach my goals while in graduate school. I will finish graduate school with no regrets. I will have gained experiences and contacts that will increase my access to greater projects and opportunities after graduation.

I will never keep a job I dislike or that makes me unhappy. I will do my best to find alternative employment and never let myself feel defeated, ineffective, or worthless.

I will produce a film encouraging stronger communication methods between scientists and the community.

I will strongly consider writing a book. As a storywriter I will remember the improv rule of affirmation and adding on to make interesting and compelling stories.

I will continue reaching for new goals. I will run another half-marathon or a longer distance. I will learn something new every day. I will listen to NPR TED Talks, Freakonomics, and other mentally inspirational podcasts teaching me new things.

Spiritual: I will spend more time outdoors. I will visit the beach at least once a year. I will worship and praise the natural creations and systems of the world. As an individual I will take all necessary actions to protect them and to be an excellent example for others. I will act in ways that make my family proud and that honor family names. I will remember the positive effects my grandfather had on society as a scientist. I will be loyal and trustworthy to my family, friends, and colleagues.

I will keep necessary "me" time to remain properly balanced and give time for self-evaluation.

I will avoid using crude, inarticulate language. I will be more polite and ladylike, and I will improve upon my posture.

I will not preemptively judge others. I will not destructively gossip about others. If I do not get along with someone else, I will try to help the relationship only positively and will avoid any negative interactions.

I will aid in the advancement of science in society. I will support the cause of using knowledge to better improve lives and the environment.

Personal Mission Statement of a College Senior

I want to live a simple life where I feel fulfilled and happy. I want to be the best possible friend, sister, daughter, and wife. I want to maintain a balanced life where I am able to enjoy both work and play and am able to let myself relax. I want to push myself to do well in my career without dwelling on failures. I want to live a healthy life where I can be happy with who I am and proud of my accomplishments.

I want to help those I care about. In overcoming many challenges already, I've gained a lot of insight into what is important in life and how to deal with complex issues. I want to be the person my friends and family come to when they're upset or happy. I want them to feel comfortable being vulnerable with me, and I want our relationships to grow. One of the best feelings in the world is helping those I love work through problems.

Although I want to have a long and successful career, I do not want my life to be ruled by the chase for perfection. I want to be able to push myself and continually grow and learn but, more importantly, I want to be able to accept my flaws. I do not want to be controlled by the anxiety I feel when I perform less than perfectly. I don't want to measure my happiness in numbers like salary or weight, but rather by my relationships and fulfillment.

Renewal and Self-Development

I need to focus on taking care of myself first before I can achieve my goals. This involves many things but can be narrowed down to four core categories: Physical, Social/Emotional, Mental, and Spiritual.

Physical: I will work to be physically healthy while not obsessing over my weight. I will make sure my body is strong, and continue to swim, run, and/ or lift weights at least five times per week. I will appreciate my body for all the amazing things it does and not judge my body or compare myself to others. I will let myself take rest days and listen when my body is tired. I will push myself and be proud when I can lift more or run faster. I will eat healthily but allow myself to indulge. I will be more vigilant to take calcium to try to reverse my osteopenia and prevent osteoporosis. I want to be healthy and strong until old age, so I need to take care of my body and treat it with respect.

Social/Emotional: I will push myself to be more social and reach out to friends. I will work hard to maintain relationships with friends and will accept social situations that don't go as I planned. I will do my best not to fear rejection in social situations and to push myself to be fearless. My emotional health is also obviously very important. I will continue to talk openly with my fiancé and to try to be more open about my feelings with others. Primarily, I will work on reaching out to people and on nurturing old and new friendships.

Mental: I will continue to work to strengthen my memory (which is damaged). I will do mental acuity exercises and work on reading more. My goal is to read more and watch less TV.

Spiritual: Although I am not at all religious, I try to live my life by the guideline "treat others as you would like to be treated." I will work harder to devote more time to volunteering. I also will try to be friendlier to those around me, even strangers. I also will try to better understand the religious beliefs of those I care about.

Roles

Learner: I've seen many friends graduate and fall into the habit of just going to work and of having fun only on the weekends. Although nothing is wrong with this per se, many feel a lack of satisfaction in their lives. I want to make sure I continue to focus on self-improvement, even when I'm not being graded in school. I want to continue to take classes, even if they're not academic (such as painting or sculpture). I never want to stop learning. I want to make sure that I continue to read and write and to nurture myself. I want to be working continually on improving myself.

Wife: I want to be the best wife I can be. I will work to be as generous and loving as my fiancé. I will make sure that we continue to talk about our issues, to be vulnerable, and to be open and honest about everything. I will do everything I can to make sure we are both happy, even when it means making hard sacrifices. I will be honest about when I need help or when I'm not happy. And I will not try to hide my feelings, being sure to reach out and ask for support. I will work to keep my body and mind healthy and to help James be as healthy as possible as well. I will make sure I don't stretch myself too far though (in my career and other commitments), so I can be sure to dedicate the time to my fiancé that he deserves.

Friend: I want to be the best friend possible. I've had a lot of great friends, and I've lost a lot a friends. I want to make sure I'm continually reaching out to those I care about, maintaining ties. Although I don't have a lot of close friends, and probably never will, I want to focus on continuing to bond with those I care about most. I will reach out to those I care about at least once every two weeks, even if it's just to check in. I will make sure they know I care about them, and I will always offer to help. I will make an extra effort to see or talk to them as much as possible and make sure they know that I'll always be there for them.

Creative Being: I fell in love with photography in the darkroom. The process always seemed so magical, and I loved how unique each image was. I used to take the time to go around the city almost every weekend and take photos. I'd hike by Great Falls or wander around downtown. Since I've been at AU, though, I haven't had as much time to continue using this creative outlet. Rather, I haven't been making it a priority to nurture my creative self. But photography is very important to me. It relaxes me and helps me express myself, so it needs to be a priority. I will focus on making the time to go out and shoot at least once a month. I will try to use a public darkroom to make sure I can continue to enjoy film.

Advocate: Having seen firsthand how mental illness destroys individuals and families, I will always be an advocate for better research in mental health. I want to help raise money for eating disorder awareness and create a film to educate others about the disease. I want to stop being ashamed of my past and use the experience to help others grow and recover. I will try to talk openly about the experience, which also will keep me accountable to my health. I will reach out to others who are struggling and try to help them. I will work to reduce the stigma around mental illness through storytelling.

Chris Palmer's Personal Mission Statement

Just for the record, and in case you're curious, here is my personal mission statement:

I want to be remembered by my family, friends, and colleagues as a person grounded in decency, simple goodness, infectious vitality, and inspiring enthusiasm; as someone with a lasting and wonderful marriage, a great sense of humor, and a strong work ethic; as a man who made his role and responsibilities as a father and grandfather one of his highest priorities; as a person who committed himself to learning and education and who pursued his accomplishments with passion; and as a man who left the world a better place.

I will live a principle-centered life, committed to personal improvement and devoted to my family and to my role as a husband, father, and grandfather. I will be a wise, dynamic, and inspirational leader whether as a father, grandfather, professor, filmmaker, environmentalist, animal-welfare advocate, author, speaker, or organization leader.

I will not let circumstances, feelings, old habits, or past conditioning determine my response to challenges. Rather, I will live according to the commitments and values I have articulated in this personal mission statement, including constant improvement in all the domains of my life, both personal and professional.

I will set and achieve ambitious goals. I will raise my productivity to extraordinarily high levels. I will find serenity while accomplishing great results.

I will continue learning that all true and lasting change occurs from the inside out. Instead of trying to change a situation or person, I will look to myself first for change. I will become the change I want to see in the world and improve myself before I try to improve others.

I have organized my personal mission statement into seven roles (or responsibilities) described below. In my weekly planning, I will fill the upcoming week with activities and meetings that derive directly and explicitly from these seven roles.

First, my role as a person who recognizes the importance of renewal and self-development: The first and most important role in my life is renewal and self-development, the vital process of enhancing my capacity to make me a more effective and fulfilled person. I have to take care of myself before I can take care of anybody or anything else. This role encompasses four dimensions: physical, social/emotional, mental, and spiritual.

Physical: I will exemplify peak vitality and outstanding health. My sixty-minute-plus daily exercise regimen focuses on strength, endurance, flexibility, balance, and posture. I will feel vibrant and have the energy to take care of my family, friends, and colleagues. I will move as much as possible to an organic, plant-based diet to avoid malnourishment and toxic food. Because my father died of prostate cancer, I have to accept the reality that in all likelihood there are malignant cells in my prostate. I will maintain an aggressive prostate cancer treatment regimen (through diet and exercise) and in the process reduce my risk for virtually every other age-related disease.

Social/Emotional: In both my work and personal life, I cannot do anything without other people. Relationships are not just vital—they are everything. I want to feel deeply connected to my family and friends, to make real and authentic contact with people, and to seek first to understand, then to be understood. I will be a source of laughter, fun, learning, and inspiration to people, and I will be loyal to those absent.

I will build my relationships with other people, especially the people I am closest to, by being trustworthy and sincere. I will do this through small kindnesses and courtesies, keeping promises, making offers, clarifying and honoring expectations, and displaying integrity and loyalty. I will do these things unconditionally and sincerely, expecting nothing in return. I will observe and draw attention to what people are doing right, and I will praise with specificity.

When I have a problem with somebody, I will focus on how I am contributing to that problem and what I am doing to help create it. Problems are, in fact, opportunities to build relationships with people faster than usual.

When I listen to people, I tend to interpret their words and feelings to fit my own opinions and experiences—as if I know the inner terrain of the person when, in fact, I don't. I will recognize this impulse and use this understanding to help develop the skill and habit of empathy. I will learn to listen to people's unspoken concerns without making judgments or giving advice. I will place myself within the other person's frame of reference in order to experience his or her feelings as that person experiences them. I will try to understand deeply the other person's point of view. In fact, I will do my best to express the other person's point of view better than he or she can.

Mental: One of the secrets of a successful and fulfilling life is continuous learning. I am committed to continuous learning and improvement and to using this learning to open up new possibilities for others and for myself. I will find mentors and drink deeply from inspiring books and other works. I will read for at least two hours daily. Because the best way to learn is to teach, I will constantly teach others what I am learning.

I will learn the distinction between "opinions" and "grounded assessments." When I offer opinions, I will make it clear they are just opinions and worth little. Grounded assessments, unlike opinions, generate new possibilities for people. Also, they lead to action (i.e., a request, an offer, or a promise), they are confined to a specified domain, they can be supported by factual evidence, and they are based on clear and articulated standards.

Spiritual: I will find joy in designing the meaning and purpose of my life, including having close and loving relationships full of grace, unselfishness, and forgiveness. I will create extraordinary results and fulfillment. I will learn, listen, love, laugh, and leave a legacy. My life must be fulfilling and meaningful in order to make sense. I will align my daily activities with my most important goals and thereby honor all the people who have loved and helped me.

I will live by the timeless principles of human conduct that are fundamental to living a satisfying and joyful life, including service, courage, hard work, kindness, integrity, honesty, patience, self-discipline, compassion, responsibility, fairness, generosity, creativity, endurance, and tenacity. In this way, I will create a life of purpose, passion, joy, adventure, and love.

My role as a husband: Being a husband is one of the most important roles I have in my life. It is the foundation of our family's happiness. I will do everything I can to help Gail lead the fulfilling and vibrant life that she dreams of for herself. I will be loving, affectionate, considerate, gentle, conscientious, devoted, reliable, supportive, and fun. I will cherish the daily routines of the wonderful life we have together, and I will coddle and pamper her. I will be an extraordinary husband, best friend, and partner to Gail.

One of the legacies Gail and I will leave is a strong family whose members love and care for each other, respect each other, laugh together, have fun together, grow together, and enjoy meaningful relationships with each other and who have a deep sense of shared vision around our family's essential meaning and purpose.

My role as a father and grandfather: I will be the best father possible to Kim, Tina, and Jen, giving them constant love and support, always being there for them, affirming them, catching them doing "something right." Having to raise children responsibly had a huge impact on my life. Kim, Tina, and Jen remade me, and I will always be profoundly grateful to them for that. I can thank them by being the best possible father to them. I will be an inspiring example for them in everything that I do.

I will continue keeping a daily journal to celebrate our family life and keep a record of what we are doing. I will also continue to write the girls nightly letters when I travel. I will do fun and joyful things with the girls, both at the micro level (i.e., moments) and at the macro level (e.g., trips, adventures, and projects). I will continue to give the girls great memories that they will treasure long after I am gone.

We will continue to have family meetings (less formal now than when all the girls lived at home), usually in the form of relaxed conversations on the phone or by e-mail. I will nurture family rituals that bring us closer together.

I will be light, playful, accepting, trusting, attentive, respectful, and considerate. I will especially listen actively to their real concerns and help them attain what they need, but I will also encourage them to solve their own problems and accomplish their own goals. I will help them to achieve great things and to lead loving and ennobling lives.

I will continue to welcome Sujay and CJ, two extraordinarily decent and wonderful men, into our family as warmly as I would my own sons. And I will be the best possible grandfather to Kareena, Neal, and Jackson, constantly seeking to enrich their lives with exuberant love and affection, as well as exciting projects and adventures.

My role as a son, brother, and friend: I will honor the memory of my parents. I will stay in close touch with my brothers, Tim and Jon. I also will stay in close touch with my relatives, neighbors, and colleagues and nurture my large network of friends and colleagues.

My role as a person who values the miracle of humor: I will honor and embrace humor as a major part of my life. It has a power and exhilaration that can accomplish extraordinary things, such as bringing people closer together and teaching me to laugh at myself. It also can put challenges into perspective, deflate tense situations, and even activate the immune system—healing the mind and the body. Laughter is an amazing and wonderful phenomenon. I will deepen my understanding of the value of humor and become a more competent observer of the humor in the mundane and routine. I will use more humor in my journal and letters. Although I no longer perform stand-up comedy, I will use humor as much as possible in my speeches, films, books, and articles. I will write a book on the subject.

My role as a "role model" for dealing competently, gracefully, and patiently with aging and death: I will become immersed in reinterpreting what it means for someone to "retire" so it becomes an incredibly active and productive part of my later life. I want to live my life in crescendo and make meaningful and vigorous contributions to society in my old age. I will grow older with grace, dignity, and joy.

I will lead a balanced, exuberant, and honorable life so that when I die, I will enjoy the profound satisfaction of having no regrets of any kind. I will leave a legacy that will benefit my daughters and their children and grandchildren, as well as many others.

I will study death and dying and deepen my understanding of it. I realize that death is my constant companion—as it is for us all. I will let this awareness guide me to make the best use of my time and live life to the fullest every moment.

I will plan the end of my life in great detail, working closely with Gail in the planning, so that the stress on Kim, Tina, and Jen (and Gail if she survives me) is minimized. One of my greatest gifts to my family will be to usher them gently through the process of my death, so that it will be an inexpensive and positive experience for them.

My role as a teacher, author, speaker, film producer, environmentalist, and animal-welfare advocate: My goal is to be a wonderfully inspirational teacher, always available to my students, and constantly encouraging, supporting, and challenging them. I intend to provide my students a life-changing experience. I want to be renowned for my exceptional teaching skills and for getting my students actively engaged in their own learning.

By working closely with my colleagues, I will help make the Center for Environmental Filmmaking into a powerhouse of national and international influence on films relating to conservation. I will continue to establish trusting relationships with all my colleagues and help them achieve their goals. I will find ways to express my appreciation and gratitude to them.

I will accomplish my goals (and our twenty-plus projects and programs) at the Center by running a "virtual corporation" with a minimum of bureaucracy and red tape, by making judicious use of the expertise of faculty and staff, and by operating in a mood of entrepreneurial hustle, passionate enthusiasm, and high productivity.

A major part of my life is as a writer and speaker. In my writing (both books and articles) I will focus on conservation, humor, parenting, teaching, retirement, aging, and dying. I will continue to write bimonthly essays on "best practices" for *Realscreen* magazine, and I will publish my new book *Confessions of a Wildlife Filmmaker* in March 2015. Also in 2015, I will publish another book, *Now What, Grad?*

I will also serve to the best of my ability as president of the One World One Ocean Foundation, president of the MacGillivray Freeman Films Educational Foundation, and board member for fourteen nonprofits.

Overall, I will warmly embrace my seven roles with enthusiasm and love and be the best person I can be for the benefit of all around me, as well as for the natural world. I look forward to getting older as an incredibly challenging phase of my life. I will be a role model for others while having an amazingly productive and fun old age. My aim is to die with my dreams fulfilled, leaving behind an identity and reputation I am proud of, and knowing that I didn't, through timidity, apathy, complacency, or lack of imagination, let an opportunity to excel and contribute pass me by.

~

Fifty Tips for Success: A Quick Roadmap to Achieving Your Goals

Fifty Ways to Radically Improve Your Personal and Professional Life, Increase Your Productivity, and Feel Fulfilled

A Workshop by Chris Palmer
School of Communication, American University

All successful people are highly fulfilled and productive. They are good time managers and are well-organized. They get a lot more done than the average person. This workshop will focus on fifty ways to radically improve your success and productivity (i.e., to get your life in balance, to focus on what's important, to get more done, and to get it done faster).

Rethink Your Life
1. *Choose the life you lead.* Improving your success involves more than ridding your life of time wasters such as poorly run meetings, interruptions, and gossip. Radical gains in success and productivity come from ceasing to pursue a course of action (a job, a contract, a career, or a relationship) that is wrong for you. Don't waste years of your life working at something that you don't particularly enjoy and that you think is basically stupid and trivial. If you are unhappy or feel unhealthily stressed, you may need to rethink your whole life rather than trying to make relatively superficial improvements.

2. *Find out who you really want to be and what you really want to do, and then align that with work you truly love.* This approach is the key to creating a happy and successful career. It will unleash untapped creative powers within you and lead to a leap in productivity that will astonish you.

3. *Don't let time, money, and fear stop you.* What can you imagine doing if time, money, and fear were not obstacles? What would you do if you knew you could not fail? If you had all the money in the world, what would you do for free? What are you passionate about? What fascinates you? What drives you onto your soapbox?

4. *Focus on what matters most to you in your professional and personal life.* Is there alignment between how you spend your time and what is important to you? Or are you spending time on projects and relationships that in the long run don't matter to you? When there is congruence between how you spend your day and what matters most to you, then you increase your inner sense of peace as well as your productivity. You feel happier, more effective, and more fulfilled. You will have both ambition and serenity.

5. *Identify the challenges you face in achieving your goals.* To repeat, do you see a significant gap between how you spend your time and what is most important to you? What things in your personal and professional life are stopping you from spending time on the issues, relationships, and projects that you care most deeply and passionately about? What is missing in your life right now?

6. *Create a list of the ten steps you can take to begin to overcome the challenges you identified in answering the last question.* A few examples might be: get a coach; identify a role model; stop smoking; eat more vegetables; be less anxious; have a weekly date with your spouse; exercise every morning; enrich your vocabulary; read deeply; be more patient with your children; get home every night for family dinners; join a cycling club; clear the mess off your desk; be more loving; get out of debt; lose weight; watch less TV; be more curious and creative; speak up more in staff meetings; get more sleep; invest in a home security system; eat less junk food; volunteer for a local nonprofit; stop to smell the roses; spend more time outside; take art lessons; smile more; keep the promises you make; make more offers; and seek help more often.

7. *List the top ten things that deeply matter to you and that are most important to you.* Possibilities include: values such as kindness and consideration for others; certain relationships; your health; having enough money to support your family; feeling useful and appreciated; living to your full potential; finding a partner; being more knowledgeable; changing

the world in some way; changing yourself in some way; working with colleagues who are decent, moral, and trustworthy; saving the environment for future generations; having more fun; being more playful; developing your sense of humor; feeling more joy in living; feeling safer and more secure; balancing your work and personal life better; getting in better shape; securing a qualification of some kind; discovering something you feel passionate about; being better organized; transforming an embittered relationship into a loving one; caring for someone you love dearly; getting out of the rut you feel you're in; feeling less lonely and isolated; being more expressive and demonstrative; and feeling more grateful for all you have.

Set Goals and Create a Personal Mission Statement

8. *Make one of the roles in your life self-development/renewal.* You have to take care of yourself before you can take care of anybody or anything else. Self-development/renewal is the vital process of enhancing your capacity to make yourself a more effective and fulfilled person. Self-renewal has four dimensions: physical, social/emotional, mental, and spiritual:

- *Physical* includes fitness, exercise, strength, flexibility, endurance, eating healthily, getting enough sleep, and deep relaxation.
- *Social/emotional* includes love, friendship, connecting with others, volunteering, helping someone, and having a sense of belonging.
- *Mental* includes learning, studying, reading, visiting museums and science centers, solving puzzles, writing, and developing intellectually.
- *Spiritual* includes finding a purpose and meaning in your life through such things as service to others, art, contemplation, poetry, going on a personal retreat to reflect on your life, creating a personal mission statement, being at one with nature, identifying long-range goals, studying your family history, leaving a legacy—or whatever ways create joy and passion for you personally.

9. *Identify the most important roles in your life.* "Roles" means your key responsibilities and relationships. For example, sister/brother, husband/wife, mother/father, son/daughter, grandparent, friend, mentor, role model, team member, communicator, educator, volunteer, manager, lobbyist, community activist, yoga instructor, soccer coach, learner, artist, athlete, entrepreneur, environmentalist, and so on. Pick no more than seven. By identifying your roles, you create a variety of perspectives from which to examine your life to ensure balance.

10. *For each of your roles, identify the people who are most important to you.* Nothing is more important in our lives than the relationships we build with other people. Relationships are everything.

11. *Select one person with whom you have a critically important relationship.* What are the assessments you would like this person to make about you at your funeral? What character traits and behaviors would you like them to praise and be grateful for?

12. *Create your own unique personal mission statement.* Your personal mission statement helps you decide at critical moments in your day what to do with your time and energy. It describes what kind of person you want to be and what you want to achieve in your life. It can be as short as one sentence, and it doesn't have to be perfect. There is no "correct" way of doing it, and you can revise it as often as you want. Without a personal mission statement, our lives can sometimes seem chaotic, overly busy, and adrift.

13. *Keep your life in balance.* The main reason for becoming more productive is so you can spend more time on what is really important to you. It is tempting to become so preoccupied with work that we lose sight of why we wanted to become successful at work in the first place. Keep your life in balance by being aware of all your important roles in your life (not just your roles at work). Having a happy home life should be among your highest goals in life. However important your work is to you, there are things in your life outside of your work that need a lot of your time, including your spouse, your children, and your health. Restorative rest, relaxation, and leisure are important. Athletes don't train all day every day.

14. *Give your life purpose and meaning.* Having a personal mission statement that is deeply meaningful to you will give you a sense of purpose and meaning. It will help you figure out what you want to do and then to integrate it into your daily life and decisions. Don't expect an epiphany as you think about your purpose in life. It often takes time to find the words for a personal mission statement that inspire and excite you.

15. *Write the story of your life.* In creating your personal mission statement, you are beginning to write the story of your life. What gives your life meaning? What should you do with your life? Who do you want to become? Who are you? What do you stand for? What is your life fundamentally about? What matters deeply to you?

16. *Set goals.* This is a powerful process. Without goals, our lives are essentially drifting without focus. Goals turn our dreams into reality.

They cause us to stretch and grow in new ways. In fact, what you *get* by achieving a goal is less valuable than what you *become* by achieving that goal.

17. *Put your goals in writing.* Your goals are of little help unless they are in writing. Putting your plans on paper makes a goal more concrete, meaningful, and real. Writing your goals makes you much more likely to exercise integrity and to fulfill the promises you make to yourself and to others.

18. *Articulate your long-range goals in your professional life, your personal life, and in the four "self-development/renewal" areas (physical, emotional, mental, and spiritual).* This step is critical if you are to align your daily activities around what is most important to you. Incorporate your long-range goals into your personal mission statement.

19. *Subdivide each of your long-range goals into more manageable shorter-range goals.* Think of these short-range goals as commitments. They must be expressed in such a way as to meet the SMART test (i.e., they must be Specific, Measurable, Attainable, Realistic, and Time-sensitive).

Plan

20. *Plan weekly, not daily.* Planning daily is problematic because it is too easy to get caught up in the minutiae of urgent activities and lose the connection between your commitments (your important strategic goals) and the daily rush of meetings, phone calls, e-mail, and so forth. Have a regular time once a week (I do it on Sunday evening) when you review your personal mission statement and your commitments. Block time on your calendar for working on these items. In this way, you put the "big rocks" on your calendar first, so that they don't get squeezed out by the unimportant "pebbles." For example, if one of your commitments is "to repair a strained relationship with a colleague," then at the start of the week schedule time (perhaps lunch) with that person. In this way, you can begin to spend more time on those relationships, projects, and goals that matter most to you.

21. *Incorporate your commitments (including those relating to renewal) into your weekly schedule.* I am repeating the previous point, but it needs to be repeated because so many people underestimate its importance. What commitments do you want to add to your schedule as you do your weekly planning? Select commitments from each of your roles (including "self-development/renewal") and make a specific appointment with yourself during the week with a determination to make massive progress on the task/relationship/project you've selected.

These "rocks" will form a solid foundation on which to build your weekly activities and help keep your life in balance. As things come up during the week, prioritize and schedule around your goals.

22. *Get a planner or notebook in which you can keep your personal mission statement, your roles and key relationships, your long-range goals, your commitments, and your schedule.* Identifying what you are passionate about and committed to achieving in your life and then keeping those commitments is deeply satisfying. A planner or notebook can help. Label your notebook or planner "My Life Plan." Mastery of the principles taught in this workshop can be applied to any productivity tool of your choice.

23. *Don't be a slave to your plan.* It isn't necessary always to follow a plan exactly. A plan is there to keep you *headed in the right direction*, not to deprive you of all spontaneity. In fact, one of the benefits of planning is to free you up to be more spontaneous and to enjoy life more. A plan gives you an option to choose from.

24. *Remember that each day is important and should not be wasted.* Each day that passes means you have one day less to live. The secret of your life and your future lies hidden in your daily routine. Derive what you are committed to do on a daily basis from your commitments in your personal mission statement rather than from the torrential flood of e-mails, meetings, interruptions, and so on that tend to distract you from keeping focused on what matters most to you. Thus, you can live each day by being true to your values, goals, and passions. Your goal is to make daily decisions consistent with your commitments. You have integrity when your daily actions are consistent with your personal mission statement.

25. *Strengthen your self-respect and integrity by making and keeping promises to yourself and others.* Making promises and keeping them (or, at a minimum, effectively managing them) is a characteristic of successful people. Take all your commitments, however small, very seriously. When you agree to do something, do it—and do it when you said you would in the way you agreed to do it. Develop the habit of attaching great importance to the commitments you make to yourself and to others.

26. *Don't let urgent matters displace important matters.* A personal mission statement helps to prevent this from happening. Unimportant but urgent matters (e.g., interruptions, some meetings and phone calls, other people's minor issues) should never be given priority over important yet not urgent matters (e.g., planning, preparation, pre-

venting crises, getting feedback, building relationships, reflection, learning, personal development, seizing new opportunities).

27. *To repeat, don't confuse urgent tasks with important tasks.* Occasionally urgent tasks are important. More often, urgent tasks are not important and important tasks are not urgent. This is why important tasks, such as building a relationship with your spouse, often get neglected.

28. *Listen attentively and actively to other people.* Most of us have never learned how to listen so that we deeply understand another human being from that individual's own frame of reference. Listening in this way is hard work. It means listening with the intent to understand rather than reply. Listening empathetically in this way doesn't necessarily mean you agree but simply that you understand. Because the other person's need to be understood is satisfied, you are more likely to be listened to and understood.

29. *Don't blame others when things go wrong, but instead focus on how you contributed to the breakdown.* When something goes wrong, it is tempting to look for someone or something to blame. A better first step is to ask yourself, *How did I contribute to this breakdown? What did I do to help bring about this state of affairs?*

Take Action

30. *Relentlessly take new actions.* In order to be successful in any field, you must relentlessly take new actions. Your enthusiasm can energize you to take action, but taking action can also increase your enthusiasm. Many of us are stuck in "inaction" because of fear or some other reason. Overcoming fear and taking action can change our mood from one of resignation and despair to one of ambition and serenity.

31. *To repeat, overcome fear and take action, no matter how small.* Taking action, even if it is only calling a friend for advice or visiting a website, gets you out into the world where good luck is more likely to happen. Thomas Jefferson observed that the harder he worked, the more good luck he seemed to have.

32. *To repeat yet again (because of its importance), take initiative constantly.* Highly productive people are intensely action-oriented. Be constantly in motion. Relentlessly take initiatives to get the job done and to move continuously toward your goals. Remember Lincoln's frustrations with General George McClellan in the Civil War. Lincoln complained McClellan had "the slows." Don't have "the slows." Be action-oriented. Seize opportunities quickly. Make requests, promises,

and offers as often as possible. Take the initiative. The faster you move, the better you will feel.

33. *Move quickly and develop a reputation for speed and reliability.* Take important phone calls immediately. Complete all small jobs (under a couple of minutes) immediately. Respond quickly to requests from people with whom you have important relationships (your spouse, your boss, your children, and so on). Pick up speed. Hustle. Do it now. Develop a fast tempo.

34. *Repeatedly ask yourself the following question: What is the best use of my time right now?* This is a key question if you are interested in improving your productivity. Discipline yourself to work only on the answer to that question. Reminding yourself that the answer is not "refreshing my Facebook newsfeed" or other time-sucking activities will help you remain productive on the computer.

35. *Apply the 80/20 Rule—that is, 20 percent of the things you do will account for 80 percent of the value of all the things you do.* Your job is to identify those few activities that are so vitally productive and spend more time on them.

36. *Always think on paper.* Don't work out of your mind. Work from written lists. Whenever you have a new task, add it to your list. Don't keep it in your head. This will sharpen your thinking and increase your effectiveness and productivity. Crossing off items one by one will motivate you to keep going, give you energy, and elevate your mood.

37. *At the start of each day in the office,* select the most important and valuable strategic task you are facing and work on that until it is finished. This will energize you for the whole day and make you feel like a winner. By starting your day tackling the biggest challenge you face, you will set yourself up for the rest of the day to storm through it brimming with self-confidence and enthusiasm.

38. *Don't waste time starting and restarting a task.* Select the most important item on your to-do list—the one that will make the biggest difference to your life and career. Then focus on it with energy and concentration. Keep only that task, and nothing else, in front of you. Discipline yourself to stay with it until it is complete. When it is complete, you will feel a rush of good feelings (high self-esteem, joy, well-being, optimism, tranquility, and high energy) that will reward you for your self-discipline.

39. *Learn to decline requests from others.* Sometimes the best time-saver of all is the word "no." How to decline a request without damaging a relationship is a learnable skill. Identifying activities in your life that

are not important to you is key to improving your productivity and happiness. What can you stop doing so you can free up time to do more of the things that are really important to you?

40. *Organize your workspace.* People who claim they work better from a messy desk are deluding themselves. Studies show this belief to be untrue. Work from a clean desk and clean workspace.

41. *Handle each piece of paper once.* Don't pick it up and then put it down aimlessly on your desk. Toss it, refer it to someone else, take action on it, or file it. When in doubt, throw it out. If you haven't read it in six months, it is junk and should be tossed. The same rule applies to e-mails: respond, file, or delete. Do not let e-mails accumulate.

Some Final Thoughts

42. *Use travel time productively.* Too many of us squander travel time needlessly. Turn your car into a learning machine (i.e., a college on wheels) by playing tapes that teach you skills you need to succeed in your relationships or some other area in which you are striving to do better. On a plane, don't drink alcohol or waste time reading the junk in the seat pocket in front of you. Rather, make every minute count by preparing for your upcoming presentations and meetings or by working on a high-priority strategic goal.

43. *Resolve to be efficient and not to waste time.* Commit to being highly productive and efficient in everything you do. Become an expert in time management and personal productivity. Learn and practice the fifty suggestions in this workshop so they become habits. Become a model of self-discipline—the ability to make yourself do what you should do when you should do it whether or not you feel like it.

44. *Make a commitment to deepen your understanding of success and fulfillment.* They are not the same. Success and happiness are not goals to capture and hold. They happen incidentally while you are living out your own vision of life and living a life built on integrity, trust, courage, love, fairness, service, patience, self-discipline, responsibility, generosity, hard work, and tenacity. Happiness is not a goal but rather a consequence of pursuing something deeply meaningful to you.

45. *Commit to dig more and more deeply into yourself to find out what you care passionately about and what matters most to you.* Implement a planning system for yourself that helps you spend more time on those relationships and projects that matter most to you.

46. *Twice a year, keep a time diary for a week.* Review how you are spending your time and compare it to how you would *like* to spend your time.

47. *Keep a personal journal.* This will help you become a more skillful observer of yourself and become more self-aware of the identity you create for yourself with other people. If you are unhappy about something or if you are pleased by something you have accomplished, write about it. When you gain an insight, put it on paper. Keeping a personal journal encourages you to improve constantly, to raise your standards, to live more purposefully, and to observe with fascination how much of behavior is "automatic" rather than intentional. Keeping a journal helps you to design and invent your own life rather than drift along under the influence of your genes and environment.

48. *Rid yourself of any duplicity in your life.* Fulfillment and duplicity are mutually exclusive.

49. *Reach out to friends and colleagues for feedback and coaching.* Everyone needs a coach. We all need help and guidance in the different domains of our life, including our personal lives. Without feedback, we stop learning and can become arrogant, isolated, and prone to errors of judgment. Your coach (or a good friend) can hold you accountable for the promises you make. A coach is someone who poses questions for clarification, challenges and advises you, provides a different and fresh perspective, listens and understands you, offers a reality check, instills confidence, and ensures that you follow up on your commitments.

50. *Reinvent yourself every year when you rigorously reevaluate and revise your personal mission statement.* Thinking periodically how you would reinvent your life is crucial to radically improving your success, fulfillment, and productivity. Do you want to continue doing what you are doing? You are getting older, and time is running out. Be bold in your thinking.

Question: What specific steps are you committed to take in the next forty-eight hours to start making changes in your life to implement what you have learned in this workshop?

Index

~

About the Author

Chris Palmer is a professor, speaker, author, and environmental/wildlife film producer. During the past thirty years, he has spearheaded the production of more than three hundred hours of original programming for prime-time television and the giant-screen IMAX film industry. In 2004, Chris joined American University's full-time faculty as Distinguished Film Producer in Residence at the School of Communication. There he founded, and currently directs, the Center for Environmental Filmmaking. Chris also is president of the One World One Ocean Foundation and the MacGillivray Freeman Films Educational Foundation, both of which produce and fund IMAX films on conservation.

Chris is the author of *Shooting in the Wild: An Insider's Account of Making Movies in the Animal Kingdom* (2010) and *Confessions of a Wildlife Filmmaker* (2015). He is a frequent keynote speaker at conferences and film festivals and regularly gives workshops on a variety of topics, including how to improve radically one's success and productivity, how to live a balanced life, how to raise money, how to give effective presentations, how to network effectively, and how to motivate and engage students.

He can be reached at palmer@american.edu and at (202) 885-3408 at American University. His websites are www.ChrisPalmerOnline.com, which contains scores of free handouts, and www.environmentalfilm.org. He blogs at soc-palmer.blogs.american.edu/.

Chris encourages you to write to him with suggestions for the next edition of this book.

All proceeds from the sale of this book will go to fund scholarships for students in the American University School of Communication who have overcome, or are overcoming, challenges and adversity in their lives, such as poverty, marginalization, racism, or personal tragedy.

Lightning Source UK Ltd.
Milton Keynes UK
UKOW04f2349151217
314508UK00001B/57/P